The Garden at Old Thatch

Victoria Connelly

Cover design by Celia Hart
Photos copyright © Roy Connelly and Victoria Connelly

Published by Suffolk Bunch
an imprint of Cuthland Press

ISBN: 978-1-910522-22-6

To Lyn and Anna-Louise with love

Introduction

Three years ago, my husband Roy and I fell in love with a five-hundred year old thatched cottage in rural Suffolk. We didn't mean to. We were actually looking for a farmhouse-style property with large, practical rooms and a solid tile roof, but there was something so special about Old Thatch. It seemed to wrap itself around us just as the garden wrapped around the old house.

Ever since I can remember, I've loved gardens and I've been lucky enough to own homes that have always had an outside space which I can enjoy – whether that's by creating a brand new cut-flower garden or simply sitting in it quietly with a good book.

This is not a book about gardening. I don't have the skills nor the experience to write such a book. It's a book about *our* garden and the happiness it brings us throughout the seasons. It's about the things we've discovered in it and the things we've chosen to grow. It captures the little corners that make us happy and shares a few of the struggles we've had while creating a place that we can truly relax in.

This is also not a book about grief, but I do talk about it because, for the last couple of years, it's surrounded me, and writers tend to write about the things around them. I guess it's our way of dealing with the world, of working things out and making things right.

In the summer of 2021, my father died suddenly and unexpectedly. He didn't get to see Old Thatch other than in the photos I sent to him, but he did make a comment about us needing a gardener! He probably thought we were a little mad to take on so much work because he was never an enthusiastic gardener. He liked a neat lawn and tidy edges, and he grew a few tomatoes in the greenhouse. But that was it. Anything else seemed like work that he could well do without after a long day in his job in television.

He would have loved the walks from Old Thatch, I know that. I think of him often when I'm walking. If he was with me, what would he think of the view across the valley, the little river, the buzzards, the rickety old stiles? He wouldn't have said much because that was just the way he was. But we might have stood a while, watching a kingfisher together or listening to a skylark, sharing a moment without the need for words.

Gardening and grief. The two seem inextricably linked in my mind. I've worked through a lot of feelings in my garden. It's been there on some very tough days and has allowed me the space to heal. And I want to share that with you now – the magic in sowing, growing and simply sitting in a garden.

My History in Gardens

I was brought up in a series of little villages in Norfolk. The first home I remember well was in a village just north of Norwich. We had a bungalow on a junction with a good plot surrounding three sides of the property. It was mainly lawn with a large area for shrubs in the front and a neatly fenced back garden with a border around the edges full of nineteen-seventies favourites like lupins in rainbow colours. I remember a lot of bare soil around the plants – something I abhor today. My love of cottage gardens demands that things jostle for space and that very little soil is visible. But this garden from my childhood was all about being low-maintenance so it was mostly lawn and a few shrubs and perennials.

A move to a village on the other side of Norwich brought a different garden into my life. This one backed onto an orchard and I loved gazing into the fruit trees and the slightly wild grass beyond our own garden. There were laburnums in our plot which our parents were frantic to explain were highly toxic and not to be touched. How could something so beautiful be so deadly, I remember thinking, frustrated that I couldn't handle those beautiful yellow flowers.

We had our first greenhouse here, but I don't recall having anything to do with it other than eating the tomatoes grown there. Gardening was still rather alien to me then. I appreciated the beauty of things – I loved the sycamore tree at the front of the property and I'd delight in watching the helicopter-like seeds spiral down from its branches each autumn. I adored the perfectly round clumps of primroses and that incomparable scent of newly-mown grass. But I was not yet a gardener.

The next move was to Beech Cottage, a nineteen-thirties home near Norwich. The house was set in a third of an acre which included – unsurprisingly – many fine beech trees, all with preservation orders on them. I remember a border full of prickly acanthus plants and many rather out of control roses, and this was the first garden I began to work in, grabbing a spade and digging a little pond and trying to tame some of the wilder plants.

It was also in this garden where I revised for my O Levels and A Levels. I had a favourite tree I'd sit under and it made wading through all my textbooks and scribbled notes that bit more enjoyable.

The university years followed which meant life on campus for a little while although I did manage to escape this for one blissful year when I found a tiny apartment above a garage in a detached house in a village deep in the heart of the Worcestershire countryside. But the garden wasn't mine. I merely glimpsed it from my windows.

Then came the renting years in North Yorkshire. When I tell people I used to live in the Yorkshire Dales, I imagine they think of cute stone cottages surrounded by hills, but my administrative assistant's salary meant several years in a ground-floor flat in a converted terrace in the market town of Skipton, where I had a tiny courtyard garden. I often remember that this garden was me in miniature for I managed to fit a rabbit hutch – complete with Rosie the lop-eared rabbit – and a rose bush in a terracotta pot into it.

Once my teacher training was complete and I was working as a supply teacher, my budget stretched to a terraced home with a slightly bigger courtyard garden which overlooked allotments. It was positioned high on a road called Castle Street and the wind could be quite fierce up there. Indeed, some of my washing once ended up in a neighbour's garden and I quickly learned to peg each item out with several pegs. But I was so fond of that little garden. One of the allotment owners, Joe, gave me some marigolds which brought such cheer to the space and I still have some of those flowers today – they have travelled with me with each house move as a reminder of his kindness. I also created a tiny pond from a plastic plant pot. There wasn't a lot of room in this garden, but the open view across the allotments made it feel bigger and there was a wooden storage box for garden tools which doubled as a bench, ideal for sunny days. I also spent many a happy hour sitting on the back doorstep, reading novels and dreaming of the day when I might become a full-time novelist.

And then came London.

When Roy and I bought our first home together, we were lucky that it came with a good-sized back garden and a small front one. The front garden was horribly neglected and full of diseased roses that looked as if they'd never been fed or pruned. We quickly got to work, planting a Magnolia Stellata and lots of other flowering shrubs which brought both beauty and some much-needed privacy to the space outside our bay window.

The back garden was all lawn with a paved path, some rather dull conifers and a forsythia in each corner. Once again, we got to work, creating new beds, planting an apple tree and making an area to grow vegetables. But I was longing for more space – somewhere we could have a greenhouse and keep a few chickens. Those of you who've read *Escape to Mulberry Cottage* will know that we actually got our first ex-battery hens while still in the London suburbs, introducing them to the garden to roam free and dust bathe in the vegetable patch. And it wasn't long after we got this flock of hens that we made the move to Suffolk.

The garden at Mulberry Cottage was dreamlike after our limited space in London and we revelled in it. There were fruit trees, established shrubs, rose bushes and climbers, and we had our first greenhouse at last. We were also able to buy a long strip of meadow at the back of the garden which meant we could make even more raised beds, growing plenty of vegetables and flowers. It was our first real taste of country living and we loved it.

As well as being lucky enough to always have a garden – even if it was just a little bit of courtyard – I've always enjoyed visiting gardens open to the public. While at university, I learned to drive and then there was no stopping me. I think I visited every National Trust property within a fifty-mile radius of campus, exploring Worcestershire, Gloucestershire, Warwickshire, Herefordshire and Shropshire. But it was more about the houses in those days. The fledging writer in me was obsessed with the families who had lived in those magnificent homes and I loved nothing more than walking through a stately room, gazing up at the ancestral portraits and imagining the lives that had been lived in those plush rooms. It's still a theme that resonates with me today and I've featured many old houses in my novels from medieval moated manors to ancient priories and Scottish castles.

But today, it's mostly about the gardens for me. Indeed, I can now visit a National Trust property for the garden alone and not feel the need to step inside the house at all. If you know my novels, you may have noticed my obsession with walled gardens. They feature in several of my books and I never tire of visiting them. There's something so special about these secluded spaces. They're little sanctuaries of loveliness, shutting out the world and focusing the mind on the beauty of fruit, flowers and vegetables. What could be more wholesome than that?

I don't think my passion for gardens will ever dwindle. Each year, I get excited to discover a few more, while revelling in revisiting old favourites. There's always something new to find. A few years ago, at the height of my rose obsession, I focused on gardens famous for their roses. Then, walled kitchen gardens became my main preoccupation as I tried to teach myself the practicalities of growing food that not only nourishes, but looks beautiful too.

My love for gardens is ever evolving but a firm constant.

Meet the Old Thatch Garden

As much as we adored the garden at Mulberry Cottage, it was a little too long and thin to be totally practical and we outgrew the little house with its tiny galley kitchen. We were both now working from home full-time and felt we needed just a little more space.

I was also longing for a wraparound garden – a plot in which our home would sit comfortably in the middle. I remember one house we nearly considered in a pretty little hamlet we knew well. The house was old and characterful and it had four fabulous acres of land. It was love at first site on Rightmove. Alas, the house itself wasn't sitting among the glorious grounds but right on the road, and I really do mean *on* the road. There wasn't even a path between you and the oncoming traffic. So that little gem had to be forgotten. But Old Thatch is perfectly positioned within its plot.

Set back from the road, the front garden faces west and has a low brick and flint wall and a little wooden gate. An old brick path crumbles its way towards the front door and is flanked by lawn on either side. Two shallow borders of flowers line the wall. The garden lover in me saw all sorts of possibilities when I first visited, planning to widen the two borders and create lots of new flower beds, reinstating the cottage garden that we'd seen in old photographs of the property.

To one side of the cottage is a parking area and another garden gate leading into what we call 'The Hen Garden' because this is where our girls live. There is another lawn here, a large walnut tree, high hedges, fruit bushes and a herb patch outside the back door where the most wonderful sage, fennel, marjoram and rosemary grow. I love nipping out to cut a few leaves when cooking.

The main part of the garden is to the east, behind the cottage. The previous owners of Old Thatch had bought an extra piece of land so there is a wonderful feeling of space here. They'd planted five young trees but had left the rest as lawn. We immediately saw it as our main vegetable growing area, imagining the beds we'd create.

One of the great delights of our new garden is the old apple tree on the south lawn. Its girth is wonderfully wide, bulging in the middle like an overstuffed retiree who doesn't get enough exercise. Its branches are almost

equally thick and covered in soft moss. It's a true beauty and we speculate just how old it is.

In early spring, there is a ring of snowdrops and daffodils at its base and I envisage lying on the grass beneath it later in the year, gazing up into its green depths, absorbing all that appley goodness.

I am also thrilled to see that the ornamental cherry has heaps of pink blossom. As a romantic, I can think of nothing lovelier than a pink tree. It stands at the front of the garden next to a beautiful young apple tree and a fruiting cherry.

One day, Roy poses a question. If I could only choose between having a fruiting cherry tree or an ornamental pink cherry, which would I choose? It's a tricky one. On the one hand, you have modest blossom, but fabulous fruit and, on the other hand, you have spectacular blossom but no fruit. I ponder. Well, the birds get most of the cherries anyway, don't they? And trees don't have good fruit every single year, so I choose the pink tree!

This is, perhaps, my favourite part of the garden and I spend many summer days sitting at a little pink table under the tree's shady limbs, reading, writing and smiling.

There's also what we call 'The Wilderness'. It's between a shrubbed area and the hedge at the front of the property. There's another old apple tree here, a large compost heap, several young fruit trees and – well – a lot of brambles and nettles.

We also have a small paved area between the back of the house and the conservatory. Facing south, this area really heats up in the summer and I have a few pots of herbs here and some scented pelargoniums. We've put a favourite bench of ours here and it's the perfect place to sit with a cup of tea and a book. And Hattie, our spaniel, who likes to join me on the bench.

So, that's the garden as a whole.

Planning a Garden

Here's a little secret – I don't plan my garden to a great extent. It kind of evolves. I write like that too. If I planned a novel out in any great detail, I believe I would lose interest, declaring the story as told, and moving on to something shiny and new. Of course, you have to have a rough idea about how you're going to use a garden and where the sun is at different times of day, where there is shade, where you can easily get a hose to if needed and where free-range hens are likely to dust bathe and disturb young plants. So I talked things through with Roy and we agreed on how to make the most of our new space.

We moved to Old Thatch in the middle of March and it felt like winter with the wind coming from the north and the overcast days with grey skies and little sunshine. There was also very little rain but we were used to that having lived in Suffolk for ten years. It's one of the driest counties in the UK. This is a constant worry as a gardener and it makes conditions very tricky a few weeks later when we find that the ground is rock hard and it's almost impossible to dig the new beds we want.

It's around this time that we discover the no-dig method of gardening as championed by Charles Dowding. So we get to work. We have plenty of cardboard boxes from the move, which is the foundation of a no-dig bed, and we remove the tape from them, putting them in place on top of the grass, giving them a good water and then placing compost on top of them. It is immensely satisfying to see a complete bed in a relatively short time.

As well as six rectangular beds, we create a central circle and I plant it with tall pink cupcake cosmos. I love these friendly faces that dance so freely in the wind, their ferny, frothy stems so soft to the touch. There are also zinnias and snapdragons to plant in the rectangular beds to the east and west of the central circular one and I envisage the flowers to come with their bright colours and heavenly scent. There are squashes too and plenty of greens.

In this garden, I basically want more of what we had at Mulberry Cottage: more fruit, more veg and more flowers. And there's definitely one thing I can't live without in a garden and that's roses. You can never have too many roses. That's what I tell myself as I survey the number of pots of rose bushes I now have to plant. They include a number of mature plants we've brought with us from Mulberry Cottage: a David Austin called Eglantyne – a shell-pink beauty, soft and gentle; Alnwick Rose – a heavenly peachy pink; and Rosa Mundi – an old Gallica rose famed for its pink and white stripy petals and its golden stamens. This rose is particularly dear to me as it's been with us since we moved into our first home together in London. When we made the move to Suffolk, I refused to leave this rose behind in the suburbs and I simply couldn't leave it when we moved from Mulberry Cottage to Old Thatch. I hope it doesn't mind making yet another move. It's a tough old plant and I hope it will bloom just as beautifully in our new garden as it has in previous ones.

It will be a comfort to have some familiar flowers with us in our new garden. As with Mulberry Cottage, there are a few roses at Old Thatch, but not enough to keep me happy. There are several standards which I've never had before. There's a yellow, a white, a deep velvety red with a delicious perfume and an unapologetic scarlet. I have to say that I'm more of a pink rose girl myself, but I'm delighted to have these glamorous flowers. The blooms will look so pretty in bud vases, dotted around the cottage.

There are also a few climbers. The one at the front of the cottage is the most heavenly shell pink. It's scented and I believe it's Albertine. This is a blessing and a curse. It's one of the most beautiful old-fashioned roses and its perfume is hard to beat, but it is only summer-flowering and doesn't repeat. But it's a well-established plant and frames two of the kitchen windows so perfectly, jostling with foxgloves and hollyhocks.

The other climber is one that's practically engulfed an old shed at the back of the cottage. It has clusters of small red flowers which open to reveal delightful yellow stamens. It could be a floribunda called Altissimo that is known for its glossy foliage which ours has in abundance. It's a stunning focal point of the garden and looks particularly lovely against a blue summer sky.

There are also rugosa roses which I'm delighted to discover as I had to leave some behind when we moved and I miss them terribly. There are at least two that need to be released from a rather overgrown patch, but I can see that the pale pink one is Fru Dagmar Hastrup.

We create a circular border in between the cottage and the front wall. I want to fill it with roses in a soft peachy pink which will look so perfect when we limewash the house Suffolk pink. And I want to interplant them. There's nothing I dislike more than seeing roses planted alone – their thorny stems bare to the world and the soil underneath them exposed. So I want to have cottage garden favourites around them.

Another job I do soon after we move in is to plant out the nasturtium seeds I brought from Mulberry Cottage, choosing the end of one of the raised beds by the greenhouse. I weed the area first, noticing the fine tilth of the soil. It's a joy to get my hands in the earth again and I dream of when

these small round seeds, which are already beginning to sprout, will provide a hit of colour in the garden.

It's funny, but I've only recently fallen in love with the colour orange. I used to do my best to avoid it, apart from the marigolds I was gifted back in my rented terrace in Yorkshire. Those marigolds really brightened my little patch with their jolly faces, but they're more than just a jolly colour – they will also brighten lunch and it's wonderful to pluck a few flowers and toss them on top of a salad, which you can also do with nasturtiums. I recently discovered that nasturtium leaves are edible too and I have a recipe for nasturtium pesto that I'm desperate to try. That's what I love about the world of gardening and plants: there's always something new to learn.

It's so easy for a few minutes outdoors to turn into an hour or two. I often find myself going out to do one specific thing and then my eye catches something else and I'm soon elbow deep in a flower border or on my knees weeding a path. This happened when I took some recycling out one sunny March afternoon shortly after we'd moved in. The side gate was open and I went to close it, pausing to take a look around the front garden and, before I knew it, I was pulling juicy great weeds out of the gravel path that skirts the front of the cottage. It was very satisfying work as the recent rain made the job fairly easy, and the late afternoon sun was warm on my back.

We quickly discover that we are much more active at Old Thatch, spending far more time in the garden. This has the natural knock-on effect that we start going to bed a lot earlier – a good hour or two. We are genuinely tired out by the time evening comes round. But perhaps it's also something to do with the fact that our bedroom window faces east so the rising sun blesses us with its friendly beams, encouraging us to embrace each new day early. Whatever it is, I rather like this new lifestyle.

What I Love About Gardening

Despite some of the frustrations gardeners can face like bad weather, pests, diseases and seeds that refuse to germinate, there is so much to love about the whole process of gardening. There are so many different stages in the gardening year. There's the imagining and dreaming stage when the catalogues land in the depths of winter. There's the moment when the packets of seed arrive and you look at the colours and shake the contents, picturing your future garden.

Then, once February and March arrive, it's time to start sowing, selecting your pots and trays and making sure they're clean before splitting open that first bag of potting compost.

This is quickly followed by the heady rush of that first germination, seeing those tiny shoots pushing up through the compost. Potting on is fun too as you get to see the plant's progress with its tenacious roots developing. Finally, after what seems like an interminable amount of time and just as the greenhouse is fit to burst and you can barely turn around inside, it's time to harden off and start planting out. And what a joy it is to see the plants going into the ground, releasing their roots to the world, glorying in the circulating air and the sun upon their leaves. Watching their daily progress is always a wonder. No matter how many years you've been gardening, nothing beats spotting that first ripe tomato or that tiny golden courgette.

And then, autumn brings harvest time. The flowers, fruits and the vegetables all demand attention and there's a mad rifling through cookbooks to use up your gorgeous gluts. There's the smell of fresh produce cooking and the joy of eating what you've grown, while making sure there is plenty to put in the freezer for winter meals.

There is always lots to look forward to when you're a gardener. But it's so much more than the physical rewards of growing something beautiful, spending time outdoors and then having fresh food to enjoy. I've long been fascinated by monastic gardens. I love how monasteries place such importance on their gardens and I think that we can learn a lot from how they used them. Of course, their closed communities rely on their gardens to provide them with readily available fresh food, as well as growing herbs for medicinal purposes, but I think there's more to their gardens than the sustenance and care of the body. Gardens are natural places for meditation and slowing down. They're also great teachers – a gardener quickly learns the importance of patience and of being willing to put time and effort into something over and over again. And gardens show us the importance of being thankful and of appreciating that our hard work, the blessings of rain, sunshine and the earth beneath our feet can nourish our mind, body and soul.

For a couple of years, I joined a yoga class at our local village hall. I went there in order to stretch my aching writer's limbs, hoping the asanas would help me to loosen all the knots that had accumulated over the years. One of the things I wasn't expecting to enjoy so much was the meditation side of yoga and, although I don't go to the classes any longer, I still try to meditate.

I have to admit, it's hard for me to sit still and switch off and I really want to be able to do that. I know the benefits of mental rest are extraordinary and yet sitting still while meditating is difficult for me. Perhaps that's why I like gardening so much. Like walking, there's a kind of rhythm when you're gardening, whether you're sowing seeds, potting up, hoeing or mowing. The mind floats and you're taken out of the everyday for a while, forgetting the mundane concerns about paying bills, making that dental appointment or cleaning that neglected corner of your house. It seems a much more instinctive way for me to reach the same meditative state as sitting on a yoga mat, and it comes much more naturally to me.

When I'm gardening, the world shrinks down to a few square feet. Nothing else exists. This little patch of earth or this terracotta pot is the limit of my world at this moment. I have cocooned myself away and nobody can touch me here. I cannot see emails or texts and I am too far away to hear the phone I've left inside.

Not long after we moved to Suffolk from the London suburbs, I wrote a letter to a writer called Ronald Blythe*. I'd recently discovered his books and had fallen under their spell completely. Their gentle observations about life in a country village; the descriptions of his cottage, deep in a hidden valley; the changing seasons and his love of literature and the arts held me captive. When he wrote back to me, suggesting that Roy and I should visit, I was elated and that first visit led to many more over the years.

During one visit, Ronnie told me how he gets up at six every morning and spends an hour thinking. As someone who finds it hard to just sit, I found this so interesting. But, now that we're at Old Thatch, I am finding it a little easier to sit and think, to meditate, to let thoughts come and go, to watch what's happening in the garden. Maybe it was just a case of finding the right place where I could sit and do nothing very well. But I think it's more than that. Perhaps I'm ready at last to embrace sitting still.

There's a line in the 1970s film version of *The Railway Children* that has always resonated with me. It's when Roberta is given permission to leave the lesson her mother is teaching and go outside. Her mother sees that she is struggling to concentrate and Roberta agrees, saying she feels she needs to be alone. 'I'll be more alive in the garden,' she says. That moment has always shone out to me. *I'll be more alive in the garden.'* I always feel that way too.

But not all gardening is fun. There are some repetitive and mundane jobs that can seem overwhelming at times like weeding although, on a warm day with the sun on your back and a soft breeze in your face, even this can be a pleasure.

When a horticultural task seems overwhelming, I pick a pocket of the garden. I choose a little patch or corner and focus my attention on that. I don't have to weed the whole garden in one day, but I can take care of a little pocket of it. That's how I do it and I often find that, when I've successfully tackled one little patch, I'm nicely warmed up to do a bit more.

The thing about gardening, for me at least, is that it's my joy – my release. I try not to put any pressure on myself because I'm not doing this professionally. Other than selling a few plants at the gate or giving some away to friends, or even entering the occasional village show, there isn't any real pressure on me to make the garden perfect. Now, don't get me wrong – I love it to look just how I want it with weed-free paths, clipped edges and everything pruned that should be, but that isn't always possible when Roy and I are working on our books and paintings. We do what we can and that's enough.

* Ronnie died peacefully at his home in January 2023, aged 100.

Sowing the Seeds

Spring sowing can sometimes seem an impossible job especially if, like me, you've succumbed to the catalogues and bought masses of new seed when you've still got dozens of packets left from previous years. I sometimes stand looking through the three tins of seeds I've managed to accumulate. The large round tin holds mostly flower seeds as well as the bulky pea and bean packets. One rectangular tin is what I loosely term my 'Greenhouse Tin', and holds all the vulnerable, heat-loving plants like tomatoes, peppers, aubergines and herbs. The other houses my favourite outdoor plants like cabbages, kales and squashes. I cannot imagine a gardening year without growing these beauties.

The flower tin is by far the biggest and fullest and it shouldn't be because I truly believe that food production should be placed higher on my list of priorities than flower growing, and yet my heart cannot resist a plot stuffed with blooms and I tell myself that they are equally important for the joy they give and the very necessary food they provide for our pollinating insects. I am also learning more about flowers as food too, and trying to use them when making tisanes and cosmetics. So flowers really do earn their place in our garden and I don't feel I have to apologise for the number of seeds I have.

But the downside of having so many seeds is that, inevitably, some get forgotten and go out of date. I will often give them a chance, sowing them in small trays and waiting with hope in my heart, but they will often have expired. Others will be overlooked for a year and then rediscovered with glee the next year – like a wonderful gift.

When I'm having a little crisis, thinking I'll never be able to sow everything, I take a deep breath and remind myself that I don't have to plant or plan the whole garden all at once. I pace myself, giving myself the far more manageable task of perhaps sowing three new types of seed each day. That's doable. Perhaps it will be a salad crop, one herb and one flower. Another day might be three kinds of cosmos. The next might be a squash day with a couple of courgettes and a butternut. With just three a day, you'll have twenty-one new varieties sown by the end of a week. So, bit by bit, packet by packet, the garden is sown.

The other thing I'm trying to learn about seeds is not to get too carried away. I can sow like crazy and then, when everything starts to germinate, start to worry that I haven't actually got room to pot on and plant everything out. Fortunately, I've always loved to give plants away to neighbours and friends, often doing a swap which is fun. I've also sold excess produce at the garden gate which very often covers the cost of the seed packets of the plants I'm selling. But I find it very easy to go on sowing more and more and then neglecting what I've already got. My beautiful germinated seedlings often have to be screaming to be potted up and I shamefacedly do so, noting that they are more root than compost as I transfer them.

During the cold spring months as I sow, it strikes me that I'm so obviously an optimist as I'm sowing countless seeds for beds that don't even exist yet. But they will, I tell myself. By the time the last frost is over, new beds will have been prepared and they'll be waiting for my beautiful plants.

The first spring at Old Thatch, I find a packet of old tomato seeds. They were, I think, twenty pence in the end of season sale at a local garden centre a couple of years ago. Will they still germinate? There's only one way to find out so I scatter a good handful of seeds in a small tray of compost and pop them on a sunny windowsill. I'm delighted when three seedlings appear, then half a dozen more. Soon, the whole tray is a jungle of little tomato plants, all determined to grow and thrive.

After that, anyone who dares to visit Old Thatch and anyone we visit is given one if not two tomato plants, and a squash as we have an abundance of those too. One day, we visit our artist friend, Celia Hart, who did the beautiful illustrations for the two Old Thatch books. I take a couple of squash plants and a tomato plant with us, knowing that she has a beautiful garden. Of course, being a gardener herself, she quickly does a gardener's exchange and we come home with some chilli seedlings and three tomato plants of hers. I couldn't be happier.

Potting Up

Roy has made me a beautiful potting tray for one of my greenhouse benches, staining the wood with linseed oil to make it durable, and it's a real joy to use, making me feel like a proper gardener. I no longer have to hold a pot in one hand while stooping down to scoop compost with a trowel in the other.

Potting up is when you begin to see the fruits of your labour for the first time – which seeds have performed well and which haven't. Do you need to sow some more of something if there's time? And what's your haul likely to be later in the year? What delicious recipes will you be able to make? As a vegetarian, the combination of tomatoes, peppers and aubergines always excites me, as do the squashes I grow. There are so many ways you can use them in the kitchen, and batch baking things like ratatouille or soups or simple tray bakes is always a glorious moment in the year, especially when you can freeze so many dishes for lazy day cooking later on. I think that has to be one of my favourite things: cook once, eat twice – or even more times!

Potting up is one of my favourite jobs. It's always wonderful to spend time in the greenhouse, absorbing the warmth and keeping an eye on all the seedlings. You get very attached to them, noticing tiny changes and lamenting if a leaf starts to curl or brown or if something gets eaten in the night by some sneaky predator. You give so much time and effort to growing produce that it can seem like a personal attack when something goes wrong. You feel robbed, victimised. But it's a simple life lesson – you are not in control of everything.

The other thing that often strikes me as I hole up in the greenhouse for a nice long session is that I should, perhaps, be doing housework. There are a dozen different chores that need doing, but nothing can compare to time in the greenhouse. Housework, by comparison, seems dull and unrewarding. It's a continuous, thankless job that, if you *do* do it, will only need doing again before you know it. Whereas sowing and growing is endlessly rewarding and it certainly makes you forget all about the housework.

There is something so life-affirming about seed germination. From something so simple as a pot of compost and an unassuming-looking seed, a little miracle happens and, after a few weeks of staring at seemingly empty trays on your windowsills, you're suddenly rewarded with stately sweetcorn plants and alien-looking squash leaves and sunflowers speeding towards the sky.

'Look at this!' I'll shout to Roy, proudly pointing to a tray of feathery cosmos seedlings, imagining the pink explosion of colour they promise come summer and dreaming of those tall, swaying plants that I'll photograph and pop into vases to place around our home. I truly love it.

Wildlife and Weeds

It is becoming increasingly important – and rather fashionable – to allow our gardens to relax a little. With the recent popularity of 'No Mow May', gardeners have been relieved of the pressure to conform to having neatly-striped lawns of flowerless grass. Wildlife gardens are a joy and a blessing. Not only do gardeners gain more time and more flowers, but the wildlife benefits too.

The first spring at Old Thatch teaches me a lot about allowing nature and the garden to guide me. As I work my way around in a tidying-up session, I notice what I'm quite sure are poppies coming up against the front door. To pull or not to pull? They aren't in the right place, but I don't want to pull all the character out of the cottage garden. It's a fine balance, I guess – not to let things get too unruly and yet to let the garden breathe and find its own rhythm. In this instance, I pull the little grassy weeds up with just a few of the errant poppies, but I leave the ones that are clearly flourishing in the nearby borders. It feels like a fair and happy compromise.

One evening, I venture into the garden. It's the beginning of May and it's light now until half past eight. The hens are still out and the air is soft and gentle. I am armed with secateurs, a bucket and a pair of thick gloves. I mean business. I'm going to tackle 'The Wilderness' – the corner of the garden that is full of horrors. It's all there: nettles, brambles and goosegrass. The forager in me knows that all of these plants can be useful to a gardener in some way. Nettles make a fine, nutritious soup as well as a hearty liquid feed for plants. Brambles, of course, provide blackberries come late summer and I'm pretty sure that goosegrass can be eaten in some form, although I've not been brave enough to actually try this yet. But this part of the garden is a heaving mass of mess and it needs to be tamed a little.

It's as I'm making good progress that I hear a scuttling. I stop and wait, wondering what will reveal itself. Sure enough, a moment later, I see the chestnut back of a mouse. It slowly moves out into the open and then stops on a piece of wood, its black eyes watching me. It's as if it's reprimanding me – coming out to tell me not to be too tidy here; that this is a habitat, a home. A mouse house. I nod. Message understood.

And then I hear a cuckoo – the first of the year – and I can't help but think that gardening has such wonderful rewards like this. Not only does it give you fresh air and exercise and a sense of purpose, but you communicate with the world around you.

Another time the wildlife chides me is when I believe the front lawn needs cutting. There are dandelions about to fling their seeds everywhere. Then, early one morning, as I'm resting up against the Aga, for we still have it on because of the cold spring weather, I see a pair of goldfinches landing on the grass. They're eating the dandelion seeds.

On the south lawn, which also needs cutting, I spy a tiny purple and yellow viola, its cheeky face peeping out amongst the grass. I sigh. We cannot cut the lawns – not just yet. Everything is too beautiful and vital.

So what exactly is a weed? The dictionary definition suggests that it's a wild plant growing where it is not wanted and where it might be in competition with cultivated plants. It makes sense that a gardener should pull out weeds that are threatening new seedlings which have been deliberately planted. I understand that and I'm fairly rigorous when it comes to keeping my vegetable beds weed-free. But some websites I look up list buttercups as weeds. This seems a little crazy to me and I'm put to the test in early summer.

We are lucky to have a small village green and it's a real beauty. We watch the march of the daffodils in spring and, once they're over, the green becomes speckled with dandelions. Daisies soon join the party and, later, buttercups. It's a joy to see. Friends of ours stop by on a bike ride, commenting that the green isn't looked after, but I like the longer grass studded with flowers.

Then the inevitable happens and a man turns up with his strimmer and mower. Surely he can't be about to destroy this wild beauty? I'm not quite sure what to do. There's a part of me that wants to run across the road and have a polite word with him. But he obviously has a job to do, and what am I really going to do to stop him – chain myself to a buttercup?

It just seems such a waste to me – a waste of time, money and energy on the part of the parish council. Isn't there enough room for both people and flowers? And surely the flowers make people happy? Don't the children who visit each day with their babysitter love them? They're easy enough to step around or over or even through, and just think how delicious it would feel to walk barefoot through them – their buttery petals cool against your toes.

I watch, keeping optimistic until the end, hoping against hope that the man on the mower will leave a little strip of the flowers, a small clump perhaps. But he is ruthless in his neatness and the green is monstrously mown.

'They'll grow back,' Roy tells me.

'Yes, and the man from the council will be back to mow them all down again.'

But haven't I myself pulled up beautiful flowers from around the garden? In the summer, we find we have an abundance of mallow and achillea growing in the lawn and in our new no-dig beds, swamping the vegetables. I do my best to pull them out and then shake my head. Isn't it crazy that I'm destroying these beautiful wildflowers and then paying money for seeds to grow other flowers? Indeed, I've bought lavatera seeds and what are they if not a fancy form of mallow? The flowers are almost identical and yet mallow is deemed a weed. And I know I've grown cultivated achillea in the past. Gardening can sometimes be a crazy business.

The Traditional Cottage Garden

When you think of the quintessential thatched cottage, who doesn't imagine roses around the door? Wisteria, honeysuckle, jasmine, hollyhocks – there are so many flowers to delight the senses. The battle is between creating this vision and maintaining the structure of the building.

When we bought Old Thatch, we noticed the black band of paint around the bottom of the exterior walls. This is a common feature to waterproof the walls against the rain drips and splashes bouncing up from the ground as guttering and downpipes are not used on thatched buildings.

There is also a narrow French drain around the perimeter of the cottage. This is gravelled and is meant to be bare but, over the decades, countless plants have been placed in it which I have to say I love, but I can see that these will retain moisture and undermine the structure of the building over time. It's a dilemma. Perhaps we can come to a happy compromise, removing some plants while leaving others. For example, the glorious pink rose, Albertine, that scrambles around two of the kitchen windows has every right to be there, I believe, and evicting it would be an act of vandalism as far as I'm concerned.

But there's a group of plants that won't damage the house but only add to the beauty of the cottage garden and that's herbs. We have lots of different mints in the garden including chocolate mint – Roy's favourite – and apple mint. They are kept in separate pots because mint is famous for spreading and intermingling which causes it to lose its individual flavour which isn't ideal.

The herb patch outside the kitchen door is well-established with plants like fennel, marjoram, rosemary and sage. But I want to grow even more and we take up a small section of lawn near the conservatory and I plant chives, chamomile, lemon balm, calamint, chervil and lovage. I'm not even sure if I'll like chervil and lovage, but I always try to grow a few new plants each year.

I love the idea of creating a potager – a kitchen garden – where you mix flowers and vegetables together in pleasing rows and patterns. It would be wonderful to do this in part of the front garden where the lawn is a blank canvas. We can see from an old photo that vegetables were once grown there. Cottage gardens were originally working spaces where the residents not only grew a few pretty flowers, but also food. They were practical places with every inch put to work. The idea excites me, but do I have time to create something quite so organised?

I suppose I already do my own version of a potager – growing marigolds alongside salad, and snapdragons next to chard. It might be a little haphazard, but it gives me a lot of pleasure and the results are always pleasing to look at even if they're not in perfectly straight lines.

Summer Arrives

When we first moved into Old Thatch, it was the middle of March and pretty cold. We were expecting spring to arrive at any moment and, indeed, we had a few solitary days of sunshine and warmth. But the long, cold days continued until the end of May.

Suffolk is well known for being one of England's driest counties, which sounds great – until you try to garden. Growing seeds, bringing plants on and creating new beds isn't easy without rain. We have an outside tap, but the effort to fill watering cans and go back and forth to the greenhouse gets tiresome, and we still need rain for the rest of the garden.

We brought a lot of plants in pots with us from Mulberry Cottage and it's quite a feat to keep them happy during the endless dry weeks we experience when we first move in. The earth is rock hard and it's difficult to get a spade into it, so we struggle in our efforts to create new flower beds at the front of the cottage. Time is passing by so fast and the plants need to be in for the growing season ahead.

And then it rains. It's like a miracle. Roy has set up a water butt by the greenhouse and we listen to the merry tinkle of it filling up. We place buckets and watering cans at strategic places. I walk around the cottage and notice that the rain coming down the thatch above the porch is creating a huge puddle. I find a plastic trug to harvest the water here and it fills up remarkably quickly.

The grass looks greener; the bergenia, which has looked dry and despondent, comes back to life, its leaves glossy once again. Jewel-like raindrops nestle in the newly-unfurled leaves of the hosta plants, and the flowers of the wisteria tremble prettily as the rain cascades through it.

We quickly discover that the rain comes off the thatch at the back of the house like a beaded curtain and that you'll get a soaking if you leave via the back door.

Then, as May edges slowly into June, we are launched into summer. The first day of real warmth is heady. We take a long walk into the valley alongside the river frothing with cow parsley. We garden, we eat outdoors and we garden some more. By the end of the day, we are exhausted. Bone weary, but gloriously happy.

As the weather continues, we cannot avoid the question of when to turn the Aga off. After all, it's been on a whole month longer than we planned and the kitchen is uncomfortably warm now that summer appears to have arrived in earnest. So we make our decision and the great metal and enamel beast slowly cools down. We feel its loss immediately. Our tea towels dangle damply over the rail and our evening-chilled hands miss the warmth from the covered hotplates.

At this time of year, it is warmer outside than inside our cottage. Rather like a church, I think, remembering the number of times we've explored bone-chillingly cold churches and then walked back outside to be embraced by the relative warmth. The warmer days encourage a little laziness, particularly on Sundays. Sundays are just for sitting – no weeding, no mowing, no potting up or planting out. Just sitting. And dreaming – that's permitted. But I soon discover that sitting in a summer garden is far from passive. You begin to tune into the colours, the sounds and scents around you. It's a fully immersive experience. I watch as a fat bee hovers noisily around the ghostly purple flowers of my potted sage plant, then crosses the garden to plunder the deep secret places of the foxgloves. A light breeze dances across my sun-warmed limbs and makes the delicate flowers of the chervil nod.

There's a blackbird standing on the tallest tree in our neighbour's garden. It's a conifer and it's a favourite spot of the blackbird who comes here most evenings. But it's the first time I've seen him here in the afternoon and his rich notes fill the air. He must have a fine view up there, across the gardens and out to the fields and woods beyond. Perhaps that's what he's singing about. Or maybe he's just enjoying the summer's day as I am.

A skylark joins in the singing, but the blackbird isn't threatened by the beauty of its song, continuing his own without missing a beat.

We are truly spoilt with all the wildlife in the garden. It's mid-June when the blue tits fledge. The air is full of them and I feel as if I'm the heroine in a Disney film and that I should burst into song. They are darling little creatures, their colours muted, but you can still clearly see the vibrant blue and yellow cuties they will become.

The next day I'm under the apple tree when they arrive, playing in the bright green foliage, cheep-cheeping to one another. With the branches just above my head, it feels as if I'm wearing a very large blue tit hat.

Late one afternoon, a buzzard soars overhead, its wings not flapping once in the time that I watch it over our garden. It's the closest I've seen one to the house and the hens are free ranging, trees and long grasses making it hard to spot them from above, I hope. Would a buzzard attack a full-grown hen? Or worse – carry one off? I remember the local sparrowhawk flying off with the blackbird clutched in its talons and I know that I would defend my hens if I need to. Although the thought of fending off a large bird of prey is somewhat daunting.

But summer isn't all spent sitting under the apple tree. It's also a time for friends and catching up over a lazy lunch in the garden with big bowls of freshly picked salad sprinkled with a few bright nasturtium flowers, crunchy cucumber, bright red tomatoes, home-made hummus and sourdough bread. It's a time for discovering what we've all been up to, the conversations meandering as the day heats up, making time for a walk, perhaps, and a chance to share some of our local beauty spots.

I remember one summer when we took friends to see the mill in our old village. We had a couple of allotment beds there so we were frequent visitors. Our friends fell instantly under its spell. 'I didn't think such places existed,' they told us and, with its large pond, its towers of deep pink and red hollyhocks and its secluded valley setting, it was easy to see how special it was.

It's always fun for me to see how visitors respond to our garden. What will they notice? What will catch their eye or capture their hearts? One visitor we had – a neighbour from our Mulberry Cottage days – came in to the hen garden and made a beeline for an unkempt area behind the henhouse. I panicked, knowing I hadn't been round there for days and that it was bound to be a horrible tangly jungle. But she stopped at the tree. Ah, of course! The glorious walnut tree. The rest of the garden tour was pretty much the same with her focusing on the trees: our ancient apple was met with great approval and she adored all the cherries, recognising them instantly.

There's another friend I am a little in awe of because her garden is always immaculate with flowers planted and pruned with regimental precision, a lawn mowed with neat stripes and borders trimmed to perfection. What will she make of our blowsy, slightly out of control garden where lawn and borders blend and some areas of grass haven't been mown for over a month? Will she disapprove or will she see it through our eyes, noticing the way that the clovers, the ox-eye daisies and mallow have been allowed to return to the lawn because we've let it do its own thing, and how the bees and other insects have embraced it? I need not have feared. She adored the garden and we sat happily together with tea and cake under the apple tree as we swapped gardening notes.

Over the years, I've got into the habit of buying myself time with my writing, working extra hard during the cold, dark days of winter when being in the garden isn't always a pleasure. So, when summer arrives with its long, balmy days, I can down tools and not feel guilty. I can sit among the buttercups under the dappled shade of the ancient apple tree with a friend or two and just relax.

Sunflowers

Sunflowers, to me, are one of the great heralds of summer. I've been growing them for a few years now and can't imagine the garden without them. As long as you remember to protect the seeds from mice, they are usually trouble-free plants. I sow the seeds into individual cells in a tray and bring them into the safety of the house until they've germinated and grown about two or three inches tall. I then take them out to the greenhouse because, invariably, something else is waiting to take its place on our kitchen windowsill.

For the last couple of years, I have collected seed from our own flowers as well as sown from packets, and it's such a joy to see new plants growing. And, once you become obsessed with a flower, you begin to realise just how many varieties there are and the happiness deepens. The first year I discovered red sunflowers was particularly exciting although yellow is pretty hard to beat. Then I discovered the furry-faced Teddy Bear, and I'm sure there are lots more for me yet to discover.

I came to sunflowers relatively late in life but, as soon as I started to grow them, I was hooked. I couldn't believe how so modest a seed could produce such a giant. It was another gardening miracle.

One year, I got a little carried away and started my seeds much too early, sowing them in February on windowsills around Mulberry Cottage. By late March, they were thin, leggy and needed propping up and it was still way too early to plant them out. In May, when the last threat from frosts was over, I planted them in the garden. They were sorry-looking specimens, but I hoped that, now they were in the ground, they'd grow stronger and start looking more normal. Alas, they never really did well, producing few flowers. But I consoled myself with a later sowing and those plants were much better. So that was a lesson learnt and I never sow my sunflowers earlier than April now. That's still plenty of time for good growth before their late May planting out.

Sunflowers are now so special to me that I have made them my heroine's motif in my trilogy, *The House in the Clouds*. Abigail Carey is an artist and entrepreneur, kind of like Cath Kidston, and she is famous for her sunflower design. I'm always fascinated when a designer becomes famous for one particular thing and I imagined my heroine idly doodling a little

sunflower pencil sketch one day, little knowing it would launch a successful business.

Come autumn, I collect the seeds, not only to grow more plants next year but also to feed to the hens. But I always make sure that I leave plenty of sunflower heads into late autumn so that the wild birds can have a good feast.

When we moved to Old Thatch, one of the first things I thought of was sunflowers. There's a willow fence on the corner at the front of the cottage and I knew this would be the perfect place to plant them. They will be tall enough to peep over the fence, nodding and smiling at passers-by. The idea excited me and I was eager to see the result. I wanted it to look like one of those beautiful Helen Allingham watercolours where she has tall flowers like sunflowers and hollyhocks peeping over cottage walls.

I like to grow a few different varieties, but I'm never quite sure which is which as the labels tend to get lost once they're in the ground. Is that a 'Giant' or a 'Titan'? And does it really matter? As long as there are enough healthy plants to make you smile, that's enough, I reason.

Later that year, sunflowers majestically waving over the fence at the village, I'm rewarded by a neighbour who stops to take photos. I allow myself a moment of pride. I am now living in the sort of cottage with the sort of flowers that I myself would stop by and photograph too.

Return to Pink Thatch

We have been invited to Pink Thatch for a barbecue in the meadow. I'm excited to be returning to this special place, which I have housesat many times, and it's the first time we will be there as owners of our own thatched cottage. The last time we visited was in the midst of buying and selling. We'd found Old Thatch, but – agony of agonies – it wasn't yet ours. But, as we turn into the driveway, it feels strange knowing that we now belong to that exclusive club of thatch owners.

As usual in the summer months, I am armed with gifts from the garden: two squash plants and a sunflower. We're immediately taken to the polytunnel where we're given two chilli plants and some wild rocket. The rocket is particularly welcome as we grew it at Mulberry Cottage and I loved it but haven't got around to sowing or buying any this year.

Seeing Pink Thatch always fills me with joy and we mention how we hope to paint our cottage soon although probably not before next year. Ingilby Paints is mentioned. They specialise in limewash for old buildings and they're a popular choice with the owners of listed properties in Suffolk. We discover that we can have the same colour as Pink Thatch as the owners mixed their very own paint for their home. This news delights me no end. We have been debating the shade of pink for some time, spotting many other pink cottages in Suffolk and declaring them too dark, too Barbie-like and some just off the scale awful. So it's something of a relief to know we can get our colour absolutely right because there is no more perfect pink than the pink of Pink Thatch.

We chat over drinks in the meadow with the other guests while the barbecue does its work. Our hosts carry food from the house in a wheelbarrow, making a delightful scene as they wend their way through the long grass with bowls of fruit salad and cream.

As evening draws in and the sun descends behind a line of trees, we are given blankets to ward off the cold. It's a heartwarming as well as knee-warming touch, showing just how much thought and attention has gone into this evening. We are very lucky guests indeed.

Of course, we do not want to leave. As always happens when we come here, even now – even though we will be going back to our own glorious thatch. But we have to make sure our hens are in for the evening. We all grab something to carry back to the house and, when we enter, we are embraced by the warmth from the Aga which is kept on throughout the year, unlike ours. On cool summer evenings such as this, I wonder if we've made terrible mistake.

There's one more thing before we leave. We are given a fabulous tomatillo plant to take with us. I'm overwhelmed by the kindness of our hosts and we make them promise to come to ours for lunch very soon to see our own thatch.

Foraging

Something I keep promising myself is that I will learn more about the plants that grow in the countryside around us and I'm determined to be braver when it comes to foraging. Up until now, Roy and I haven't ventured much further than making nettle soup and blackberry and apple crumble. It's pretty basic in terms of foraging but immensely enjoyable and rewarding.

One of the first things I spotted in the garden at Old Thatch when we moved in was the patch of nettles, but it didn't fill me with horror. Rather, I felt thankful because, for the last few years, Roy has been making nettle soup. Known as 'Gardener's Revenge Soup', nettles are highly nutritious and make a fantastic base for a soup. Actually we have to confess, we may have used it for another kind of revenge too.

A few years ago, I was coming to the end of a contract with a publisher. It's always a difficult time and, to make matters even trickier, I'd lost my previous editor and been handed over to another one while in the middle of writing a novel. The first editor had green lit the novel, professing their enthusiasm and so I went ahead and finished it. The trouble came when the new editor read it and decided that it wasn't right. 'You can keep your characters,' she told me. Well, as any writer or reader knows, character *is* story. You can't just take a set of characters out and plonk them into a new story.

Things got progressively tricky, communication broke down and the editor suggested coming out to visit me at my home in Suffolk. I'd never experienced that before and I have to say I wasn't looking forward to it. We offered to make lunch and that's where the nettle soup came in. It was like a little joke – a writer's revenge of sorts. The irony was, of course, that she loved it. After all, it is very good soup! But Roy and I still laugh about the time when we fed nettles to an editor.

I find a recipe for nettle pesto, but there aren't enough new plants. The ones we have are old and tough and wouldn't make good eating in a fresh dish like pesto. So we'll wait for the second flush come the autumn. But I do want to try fresh nettle tea so pick the top few leaves from the newest plants I can find, carefully wash them and then steep them in boiling water for five minutes. The result is surprisingly good – it's a savoury sort of taste that I don't feel needs sweetening. I've read about the benefits of nettle tea and think about all the good things I'm ingesting as I'm sipping it at my desk. Nettles are rich in iron, calcium, magnesium, vitamin B and C. They are an antioxidant and are good against allergies. They're also an anti-inflammatory, so there are many benefits to drinking a cup and to not digging up your patch of nettles.

We also use nettles to make a natural fertiliser for the garden. Like comfrey fertiliser, it's very easy to make, needing only the plant itself, rainwater and a container you can close. It's one of the smelliest things ever so try and place it away from your house or, indeed, your neighbours' homes. You will not be popular if you inflict it on anyone. But I love making it so nettles are always welcome in our garden and I like that it means I don't have to spend money on shop-bought fertilisers.

We're very lucky to have a signed copy of *Food for Free* by Richard Mabey and I take a renewed interest in it now that I want to forage more. I flick through the pages, hoping to recognise things from our garden and the local hedgerows and fields. Dead nettles are edible, he says. As is goosegrass, which I knew about. We have plenty of both and I determine to try them, picking a generous helping of them for tea one day. Alas, I don't enjoy them and I quickly decide that, just because you *can* eat something, it doesn't mean that you have to.

But then I come across a plant I've been trying to identify for a few days. I've seen it on walks and there's even a little patch in our garden by the back gate. It's tall with wide leaves and clusters of small white flowers and, to my untrained eye, it certainly looks edible. So, when I spot it in Mr Mabey's book I'm delighted. It's called garlic mustard or Jack by the Hedge and can be eaten fresh in salads. It's good for people who like garlic but, for whatever reason, can't eat it. I pick a tiny piece of one of the leaves and have a nibble. It really does have a taste like wild garlic. The smell is like wild garlic too only much milder. I decide this is definitely going in dishes and, that lunchtime, I put a handful in the pesto I'm making and the result is good. I'm delighted to have this free resource.

Shortly after moving to Old Thatch, I was excited to discover Alexanders growing profusely along the roadside. This is normally a plant found near the coast so it was a real joy to see it this far inland and there is plenty of it. Every part of the plant is edible – flowers, stems and leaves. You can steam it or blanch it and eat it on its own or in soup and it has a taste a little like celery with a twist of aniseed. It flowers for weeks in the spring, but it's important to check its freshness.

I wonder about collecting seeds in the autumn and growing it in our garden. It would save worrying about pollution from traffic and pesticides being sprayed nearby, but then a friend warns me that she grew some in her garden and now can't get rid of it. It's a forest, she tells me. So perhaps I'll content myself with a few foraging trips each year and enjoy their chartreuse splendour in the wild.

Another favourite of mine is the humble pineapple weed. Growing up in rural Norfolk, I was aware of the plant for years before I knew what it was, crushing it underfoot as I walked through the countryside, releasing its sweet scent. But I didn't know until recently that it makes a very pleasant tea. I like to collect a dozen firm yellow heads, give them a wash and then use them in tea with a little squeeze of fresh lemon. It makes a lovely sweet drink and makes you feel as if you are imbibing sunshine.

My foraging is still pretty basic, I know, but I am constantly learning and honing my skills and I can't wait to discover more.

Flower Heaven

It's curious how some exotic plants from far-flung parts of the world seem so very English to us now. It's hard to imagine a quintessential English garden without them. For example, the wisteria, all the way from China, seems absolutely at home embracing an English country cottage, and we're lucky to have it growing on the east and south faces of the hip end of the cottage as well as on the west front. Its scent is wonderfully heady on warm spring days and I love gardening nearby, making time to weed the gravel path and the dahlia bed so I can inhale the perfume as I work. On summer days, you can even smell it when inside and I love looking through the jewel-like cascades of flowers from the living room as it frames the casement windows so perfectly.

In May, we discover a rather pretty plant growing under the wisteria. It has a delicate white flower and fills the border in a snowy haze – a little like a smaller, stockier cow parsley. A visiting friend, in a warning sort of voice, informs us that this is ground elder. We've never actually seen it before, but we know of its reputation and of the fearful hold it has over gardeners. However, we rather like it. Okay, so we don't want it spreading right across the whole garden, but we can keep an eye on it, can't we? And surely it would make a good filler for a vase of flowers?

Something that definitely is welcome is tulips. I discover a clump of sunny yellow ones in a border and, for the briefest of moments, consider cutting them for a vase to brighten up a dimly-lit corner of the cottage, but I resist, knowing that they will last so much longer in the garden and that I'll enjoy them all the more here, lording it over the primroses in sunny stateliness.

There are also some stunning red and yellow striped tulips hiding in a border under a rugosa rose. They look a little lost there and I wonder if I should move them at some point.

Tulips are something I've never really had a lot of luck growing. I was once gifted a bag of tulip bulbs and planted them in our London garden, not knowing I should dig the bulbs up each year, so they withered away in the thick clay. The only other tulip experience I had was when I fell under the spell of Angelique – a deeply feminine blousy flower with pale pink and cream petals. I filled a container with bulbs and took care to lift them and store them. Alas, the only place we had to keep them was the greenhouse and the mice got them. So I don't have a good track record with this flower, but I would like to try again, making the garden juicy with tulip colour, perhaps planting them au naturel in the lawn in our woodland garden where they can mix with the cow parsley and forget-me-nots.

I love how flowers mark the passing of each month – each week, really. Time passes so quickly, each day bringing new and unique joys, but I can't help wanting to slow it all down sometimes. No sooner do we get used to the fresh and vivid purple of the wisteria against its glossy green leaves than the flowers start to fade in colour and the foliage darkens, becoming almost bronze in places. Its scent is still extraordinarily powerful and has been a happy companion to me during several evenings in the garden. But how I miss it once it's over.

The lilac, too, is over in a heartbeat. Because of the wet weather, I didn't have a chance to bring armfuls of this inside, as I dreamed of doing, to dress one of our fireplaces. I pick some for a bedside display and how romantic and feminine it looks under the eaves at the top of the cottage. But these showstoppers must make way for others to entertain us and there are peonies, lupins and roses yet to come.

I recently became obsessed with heleniums, desperate to grow the tawny ones that remind me of orange marmalade. I can't remember when I first saw them – possibly on the TV – but they've slowly worked their way into my heart and, after a trip to Hidcote where there was a fine display, I knew I had to track some down. However, they weren't easy to find. I spent a good three years looking for seeds.

At last, I found a stockist, but there were none available until the spring. I wrote the details down on a bit of paper – my gardening wish list for the year and, come May, I took delivery of one. It wasn't cheap to order because of delivery charges, but I'm hoping the plant will spread in time and be a good investment.

The red hot pokers in the garden are something I have yet to make up my mind about. The previous owners seemed to adore orange spiky plants whereas I'm not a big fan. I wasn't totally sure what they were when I first saw the leaves, but I remember hoping some, at least, were irises or agapanthus. Alas, many of them weren't and, as spring progressed, they threw up their green triangular flowers. I watched as they turned orange, opening wider, pushing ever skywards. More and more of them appeared around the garden, making some of the borders look quite angry.

I had to admit that there was something admirable about their stature, their relentless upright thrust, but then they began to fade, the base of the flower turning yellow until just the top was left orange. They reminded me of Beaker from The Muppets so we kept a few for comedy value and it seemed a shame to compost them as they're quite impressive plants. But

worse was to come as the colour faded completely, leaving frizzled grey-brown stalks. I have to admit to taking a few up and giving them to friends and neighbours who are more appreciative of them than I am. I've even sold a few at the garden gate. I will spend the money on cosmos seeds, replacing spikes with froth. Still, there is plenty of room in this garden and I haven't the heart to take them all up. Besides, I've now become interested in the Victorian artist, Marianne North, who travelled the world, exploring jungles so she could paint exotic species. It turns out that there is a red-hot poker named after her. I wonder if ours is it.

We soon discover a border full of day lilies. They bloom in late June, statuesque but scentless. I love how they float above the foliage of the plants below them. But I'm not so keen on the spiky plants which we soon identify as stinking iris. In the winter, these have scarlet berries which fling themselves absolutely everywhere and the tiny plants can be found all over the garden – in the gravel, the grass and in most of the borders. Even as young plants, their leaves look scabby and I'm not keen on the spiky mature leaves either so I decide that they should all go. This is quite a job and proves a good workout. But it seems impossible to get them all in one go for they're easy to overlook as they self-seed under large shrubs, thinking they're safe from my ministrations.

Their rhizomes make me wonder if I'll ever see the end of them. I don't know anything about my enemy's underground domination and wonder who will win this battle. But it's satisfying work knowing that I'm clearing the earth for prettier plants like the hollyhocks and columbines I have grown from seed and which are waiting patiently outside the greenhouse for their time to be planted.

The circular rose bed I created at the front of the cottage hasn't quite worked out as I'd planned. I'd envisaged my peachy pink Queen of Sweden roses floating among the white cosmos. Well, I didn't do my homework properly because the cosmos I planted was Purity and, come summer, it's enormous, completely drowning the young roses so that you cannot see them at all. As a bed, it is spectacular. You can see it from across the road, the white flowers nodding and swaying lyrically in front of the thatched cottage. It is perfect for a romantic English garden and I love it, but I am anxious that my roses won't survive and whisper an apology to them, clearing a little space around each plant so it will get its share of light.

The feathery stems of the cosmos on my bare legs feel delicious as I'm cutting them back. I fill a bucket which, in itself, becomes a glorious thing so I place it outside our back door so I can see it from one of the kitchen windows. The insects love it and are frequent visitors.

A garden is never complete. There will always be something we want to add or take away. For years, I've yearned after Himalayan poppies – the summer sky-blue beauties that I've only ever seen once in real life. They are hard to grow as well as hard to find, but I finally tracked down a packet of seeds one year and sowed them carefully, giving them the germination conditions they needed. Or at least I thought I did. But not a single shoot was seen and I had to admit failure. The thing with gardening is that each year is different and, as every gardener tells themselves, next year will be even better and you can try again.

Visitors and Visiting

Summer is a time for friends and we can't wait to invite people round to the house, but there are still restrictions during 2021 because of Covid and so we're limited to being outdoors. This suits us as we're keen to share the garden and it's lovely to sit out once the weather has warmed up. One of the first people to pop round is our good friend Ellie, who we've known ever since we moved to Suffolk. She arrives with a gardener pal of hers after a trip to a local secondhand bookshop which has opened again after lockdown. Indeed, it's one of my friend's first outings in over a year as she's been isolating.

I gallop behind as the two of them march from plant to plant, nodding and naming everything. I think I remember about one in three and wish I had a pen and paper with me.

The quince tree we discovered in a corner behind the hen coop is ornamental, alas, despite its marvellous scarlet blossoms which we thought so promising of an edible harvest. I tell them our plans for the vegetable beds and more flower beds and promise to invite them both back to see our progress.

Another visitor arrives with her young daughter. Dora is four and is very lively and inquisitive. She is desperate to explore the garden and we're happy to show her around. She keeps calling my name and asking to see 'more'. But we've already seen everything. Then I get an idea. We'll walk around the garden in a different direction. Will she notice? She doesn't seem to as we set off and I remember how very small she is and realise that she will be experiencing a whole different garden from me. Our adult eyes sweep across the whole place practically at once, but she needs to move around in order to see it all.

We approach 'The Wilderness'. We've already walked through it from the other direction. This time, she declares, 'It's like a fairy world' and I see how the cow parsley towers over her in a magical froth and wish I was four again so that I could see it as she does.

Once she believes she's seen everything, we sit at the garden table eating pastel-coloured macaroons, their fruit flavours fizzing on the tongue. There are cookies too and herbal tea for the adults. It's a delicious little spread of

slightly naughty food that none of us feels like apologising for. Sometimes life needs a good injection of confection.

Over the years, we've gathered together a hodgepodge collection of chairs and benches. One bench is a delightful handmade piece by a craftsman from our last village. Another is a heavy wrought-iron bench decorated with acanthus leaves. There's also a sweet pink metal table with two chairs. Some of the metalwork is faded and the floral decoration is brittle now, but it always looks so pretty in the summer garden among the flowers and is lovely to use when friends call round.

One thing we don't have is a parasol. I inherited one many years ago, but it was badly damaged and, quite frankly, dangerous. We still have the metal stand, though, as it's a beautiful thing in its own right. But I do long for a lovely jolly parasol to read and write under when the sun becomes a tad too strong.

One afternoon, I'm musing on the subject of parasols again as my chosen corner of the garden starts to get uncomfortably hot. We recently saw a real beauty at a place that sells gorgeous home and garden ware. But it was prohibitively expensive. In the meantime, I walk across the garden to sit at my pink table which really looks at home under the old apple tree. I put my book to one side and gaze up into the dappled depths of this precious tree. Its canopy is enormous and I'm grateful for its cooling shade. And then I smile. What is this if not nature's very own parasol? What was I thinking of, contemplating buying something man-made when, right here in our own garden, is the loveliest of shades?

The Hens of Old Thatch

The garden is not just of great importance to me and Roy but also to our hens. It's their habitat – somewhere for them to stretch their legs as well as their wings when they're sunbathing. They dust bathe in the borders and forage in the lawn. And, on occasion, kick up a young plant or two. But that's a small price to pay for their quiet, comical companionship.

I love glancing out of the window and catching a hen walking by or being greeted by them when I open the back door. Sometimes, they come racing across the lawn to see me, hoping I might just have a tasty morsel of food for them. Or I'll wander outside and have no idea where they are, only to see a fluffy bottom poking out from the geranium bed a few minutes later or a hen scuttling down the compost heap.

One thing is certain – I can't imagine a garden without hens. We've had them for eleven years now and they are so much a part of our lives. We wake up knowing there will be fresh eggs, we watch them throughout the day and we make sure they're safely tucked up at night. Our day is very much linked to theirs.

For me, one of the greatest joys of hen-keeping is being able to grow food that our hens can enjoy as well as us. There is nothing more satisfying than walking out into the garden and being able to pick a handful of greens from one of the beds and feed it to the hens. It's especially gratifying on a winter's day when there is very little else growing.

Chard is a favourite of mine. It's easy to grow, has relatively few pests, is fairly slow to bolt and looks very pretty too, especially if you get the rainbow variety where the stems come in yellow, white and red. The hens adore the glossy green leaves and, once it's past its best, I dig up the massive plant and the hens get a rather long treat, tearing off the remaining leaves and leaving the thick stem. When I clear it away, I can't help but marvel at the fact that this impressive plant began as a tiny seed in my hand just a few months before. As I take the stem to the compost heap, I think about the cycle of the seasons and how the seed became a plant which fed us for months and now it will become compost which will feed the beds where I'll plant future seeds.

Cabbage is great too – both for us and the hens, and the leaves of our calabrese plants go down well with us all. Funnily enough, though, the hens turn their beaks up at cavolo nero which means there's more for us, but it's strange that they don't enjoy this particular delicacy. Perhaps it's the darkness of the leaves or the bubble-like texture which they dislike. It seems strange to me that they love the humble dandelion leaf, but won't eat cavolo nero!

During our first summer at Old Thatch, we introduce four new girls to our flock. They're ex-bats from one of our regular pick-up points via the marvellous British Hen Welfare Trust. It's always a special day on the calendar when we go to meet our new girls, taking a couple of cardboard boxes with us in which to transport the new members of our family home.

I like to name each new flock as a 'family', choosing names from a favourite book or writer. These girls will be Gwendolen, Cecily, Miss Prism

and Lady Bracknell – names from that most delightful of plays, *The Importance of Being Earnest* by Oscar Wilde. We could always refer to them as the 'Wilde Girls'.

When they first arrive and we see them properly, we notice that each is missing a fair few feathers and their combs are large, pale and floppy. But we've seen hens in much worse condition. We've divided the hen run in half so that the new girls are in quarantine for a while. Not only is this essential to avoid any potential health problems, but it's good for allowing the new girls to settle in. It's a huge change for them. They've come out of factories and have never been outside before. They'll need time to get used to the open air and having earth under their feet. They'll also need to learn where their home is and when to put themselves safely to bed. As usual, Roy and I end up helping out with bedtime for the first few evenings, picking them up and popping them in to their coop. But they soon learn.

Out of all the flocks of ex-bats we've rehomed over the years, these girls are the hardest to differentiate between. I'm genuinely struggling to tell them apart until I come to a realisation. Two of them have combs that flop over onto the right side of their heads while the other two's combs flop left. This is enormously helpful, but I'm mindful that this might change as their combs shrink a little. They are usually abnormally large due to the warm conditions of factory life and will lessen in size once the hens have been free ranging a while. Still, in the early days, I can distinguish Miss Prism and Lady Bracknell (combs to the right as you look at them) and Gwendolen and Cecily (combs to the left as you look at them).

Sure enough, as the months go by, Lady Bracknell's comb shrinks in size so that it is very neat indeed and the most upright of the flock. She is also a dominant personality so it appears we've chosen her name well. Gwendolen is also a strong personality and a bit of an escape artist. If there's the smallest gap, she will get through it, much to the annoyance of the other girls who see her wandering off on adventures around the garden while they're confined to their run.

Miss Prism is a little shy but very vocal. I can hear her plaintive calls right across the garden. And Cecily is perhaps the gentlest of them all and has potential as a cuddling hen. Early in our acquaintance, I popped her on my lap and she stayed for ages, happy to be stroked while looking at the world from her new vantage point.

Our established flock – Portia, Phoebe, Perdita and Mini P – accept this new flock without too much fuss although Portia sounds out her protest in the early days, complaining loudly at these interlopers. But we have the best integration ever with very little bullying and barely any bloodshed. We've had a few horror scenes in the past with kung-fu style battles, bloody combs and broken toenails. It's heart-stopping to watch and I'm glad we've had nothing more than a bit of comb-pulling and feather pecking this time.

Mini P is the worst bully, I notice. This is often the way with the lowest in the pecking order – which she was before the new girls' arrival. It's a pattern we've become familiar with over the years – the previous lowest in the pecking order makes sure she's in charge of any new arrivals, putting them in their place in an often brutal fashion.

But it's easy to forgive Mini P because we know what she put up with in her time and she does lay us the biggest eggs. In fact, it's one of these large eggs that causes her a mischief one day. She's not looking good – her wings are down and she's straining to lay. Roy rushes her to the vets and returns later with Mini P and the biggest egg I've ever seen. My eyes water just looking at it and I tell Mini P that she really doesn't have to work that hard – a medium-sized egg would suit us just fine for breakfast.

Not long after this, we notice that Mini P had stopped laying eggs altogether. Or so we thought until Hattie found an egg in the garden. When I first saw Hattie with it, I didn't even recognise it as an egg and wondered what on earth she had found, but I managed to get it off her, trading it for a dog treat. A moment later, she had another in her mouth. Again, I gave her a treat in return for the egg and then watched as Hattie made her way to one of the geranium beds that flanks the house. It's then that I remembered Mini P occasionally bedding down in this geranium bed and I go to investigate. Sure enough, there's another one of her huge round-bottomed eggs hiding among the pink flowers. I smile. Well, I always wanted free-range hens.

Good detective work, Hattie!

During our first summer at Old Thatch, Portia is broody. She's a Buff Orpington and we're aware that this is a trait of the breed. Indeed, we made the very best of this back at Mulberry Cottage, encouraging Portia to hatch some eggs for our farmer friend (photos of her chicks can be seen in *Finding Old Thatch*). And what a delight it was to see Portia in her natural element. There is something so special about a mother hen fussing around her fluffy offspring, teaching them how to eat, scratch for food and be alert to danger. We loved the experience. But we're not set up here for chicks and we have no cockerel so the eggs Portia is sitting on – stolen from the other hens – won't be fertilised.

I watch her closely each day – flat and golden on the deck of the coop, she sits patiently, waiting for eggs that won't ever hatch. We take her out once or twice a day to make sure she's eating and drinking and to get some much-needed sunshine on that pale comb of hers. She objects, making herself heavy and unwieldy. Once outside, she eats with gusto, but squawks and clucks and flaps her wings, longing to be back inside on those eggs.

Finally, after weeks, she's out again of her own accord and it's so good to see her about in the garden, walking through the flowers, preening and dust bathing with the rest of the flock. I've missed her golden presence. And then, without warning, she becomes broody again. It makes me very anxious

as she slowly begins to lose condition. Spending so long inside without proper food and sunlight is not good. She's losing weight and that wonderful golden brightness.

When she comes out of her second bout of broodiness, we notice that she's having trouble with her balance. Her legs are weak. We do all we can to feed her up, dosing her food with supplements and isolating her momentarily from the other girls so she can eat uninterrupted. But she goes downhill rapidly. I've never felt so helpless and distraught. This is my special girl and I love her so much. We *have* to save her.

We take her to the vets, but it isn't hopeful. They've never seen this before. I contact a friend who's had Orpingtons in the past. Again, she's not come across this. She tells us to do all we've been doing already, but Portia is becoming weaker. She's now falling over a lot and doesn't have the strength to get back up. Several times a day, I'm running out to help her. When she's down, the others tend to peck at her, spotting her weakness. Nature is cruel and it's hard to witness. We give it a little more time, but it now seems like cruelty and I know what's coming although I can hardly bare to face it.

We bring her inside and I kneel down beside her on the kitchen floor, tears blurring my vision as my heart breaks, and then we take her to the vets.

Losing Portia was so very hard and would have been enough to go through on its own but, within a fortnight, we notice that one of Portia's surrogate chicks, Mini P, is not looking her normal, buoyant, bullying self and, one morning, when I open the coop, I find she's passed in the night. It would be fanciful to suggest that she missed her mother hen, but I do believe that some hens form close bonds. I've seen them making natural pairings, but Mini P was pretty much a loner after she lost her sibling, Audrey back at Mulberry Cottage. We're not quite sure what was wrong with Mini P but, after the struggle she'd had laying enormous eggs in the past, perhaps it was related to that.

Our flock is ever-changing. A hen's lifespan can be cruelly short, particularly the ex-bats that we rehome, and my heart breaks a little at each and every loss. Each hen has its own very particular character and a special way of endearing themselves to you whether they're a friendly soul who loves a cuddle like our Primrose from our second flock of ex-bats; a cheeky elderberry thief like Ella – another ex-bat; or a placid white beauty like Peggy our Sussex Star. Every single one of them brings something unique into our lives and we love them for it.

The Walled Garden

I first discovered florist Anne-Marie on Instagram. She works in a stunning walled garden in a remote Suffolk village. She was running a course the August before we moved to Old Thatch, teaching flower arranging – A Floral Abundance day. A friend of mine was going – did I want to go too? Well, I couldn't think of anything lovelier than spending an entire summer's day in a walled garden, learning about flowers. So I replied with a very enthusiastic yes!

We're given directions and, after an unexpected detour via the roundabouts of Bury St Edmunds, we find the village. We're to look for a turn onto a track into a little wood and then a turn left before a large tree. It's a wonderful set of directions – the kind you might find in a children's adventure novel – and it really does feel like an adventure as we enter the wood, make the turn and approach a long wall. Dark trees tower above us and we make our way towards the gate.

I am instantly in heaven. It is a kingdom – a secret, magical world of flowers. It's such a tranquil space that I sink in to it instantly. There are rows and rows of long narrow beds, each filled with flowers and grasses, providing colour and texture all year round for the wedding bouquets and floral displays that Anne-Marie creates for her customers.

After a tour of the garden, a little tuition and a deliciously flower-festooned home-made lunch, we are given a big black bucket each and a pair of secateurs. Our mission? To take whatever we want to make our own displays. It is both a delightful and daunting task as we are let loose in this little paradise, each of us approaching the flowers with caution, our secateurs hovering anxiously. We are all much too gentle in our ministrations, we're told. I'm snipping the tops of flowers when I should be going much lower on the stem.

'Then these buds won't open!' I plead, motioning to the new flowers to come further down the stem. I'm told to snip. And that's where I've been going wrong for years – being too hesitant and only taking the shortest stems for fear of losing a few flowers. Thus, my arrangements are always so small. But now I'm gaining confidence as I bend down and claim my floral prize. My bucket fills. Okay, so there's a lot of pink and it might not make the classiest display, but the colours I'm choosing – the big fat, happy dahlias

– are so heartwarming. I can't resist them. I glance at my friend's bucket. Her palette is much subtler than mine with antique shades of coffee and cream. I wonder if I should change tactics until I spot another pink bloom that I simply must have.

I also meet the most wonderful plant and take some of that: Thalictrum delavayi, 'Hewitt's Double' – it's tall, its slender stems towering above me, stately and graceful, and it immediately goes onto my list of plants I want in my own garden. It's covered in tiny vivid purple flowers that are hazy and cloud-like. Once again, I feel guilty for wanting to attack it with my secateurs, but my lust for getting some into my bucket overtakes me and I make some tentative cuts.

Driving home at the end of that summer's day, the car full of flowers, I couldn't feel more content. Anne-Marie has the most beautiful workspace I have ever seen. She's created a business and a world that is both unique and inspiring. I vow to return, taking Roy with me, one day. And we do exactly that, visiting on one of those sun-drenched days in September when it still feels like summer is blessing us. It's a brief respite from a tumultuous time when we're trying to sell our house. I remember my nervous energy around then. We had found our future home, had our offer accepted and were busy booking surveys, arranging the mortgage and doing everything that needed to be done, but we still had to secure a buyer for Mulberry Cottage after our first buyers had dropped out. Time spent away from everything was much needed and I really welcomed that afternoon in the walled garden.

I am so inspired by what Anne-Marie has created and the work she does. Her Instagram feed is a joy as she shares her weekly progress. I asked if she'd tell me more about the walled garden and she kindly agreed to share her thoughts.

Anne-Marie:

I found this space, a Victorian walled garden, nearly ten years ago now. I wanted to start a seasonal, sustainable flower growing business and I had been on the lookout for a piece of land ideal for growing. When I first visited this space, surrounded by woodland, I just fell in love. It was the perfect space, about an acre, with three metre high walls giving protection from the elements (and some wildlife) with characterful outbuildings, including an old gardener's bothy and the remaining metal framework of a thirty metre glasshouse. The space has been a joy to work in. There is something quite magical and romantic about a walled garden and these walls have considerable horticultural history as well as providing gorgeous backdrops for floral photography – another passion.

The garden was totally overgrown when I first saw it and I knew it would be hard physical work to get it to be something that I had in my imagination. When I took it on in July 2010, an extremely hot summer (with lots of horseflies to share the space with) I remember that summer as a very exhausting one, trying to clear a large space of 'good enough' soil to sow seeds directly in the ground for harvesting in the following spring. I marked out the space, keeping the main crossing paths as a structure so I could work four quadrants, one at a time, so the whole space wouldn't overwhelm me.

During the main British flower season I am there, in the space, pretty much every day, weeding, picking, sowing, arranging, teaching, talking to customers, catching up with friends and family. There are so many things about this space that fill me with pleasure: the floral abundance in high summer, the variety of butterflies and bees, the tranquillity of the space and sharing it with others is a joy but, overall, the biggest pleasure is sowing a seed and letting the flower and plant tell its own story through the seasons, all the way to the final arrangement this cycle feels like a complete artwork of nature.

But there's nothing I love more than closing the gate and having the space all to myself. It is the most mindful, wholesome space I have had the pleasure of being in. It saturates my whole being and feels like a total privilege to work in, bringing life back to an old walled garden that had struggled to find a use in recent years.

Now the garden is flourishing and being used in a way very close to its original purpose. Many of the methods used would also be familiar to the estate gardeners from a century ago, providing a supportive space for a variety of wildlife as well as producing something beautiful.

You can find Anne-Marie on Instagram and enjoy her walled garden for yourself at www.instagram.com/forageforflowergarden.

The Saddest Summer

The call comes on a morning in early August 2021. It's the hospital in Norwich and it isn't good news. My father has died. He'd collapsed at home and was taken to hospital immediately, but didn't regain consciousness. He was seventy-seven. I take the news in, but don't really comprehend the weight of it.

My brother visits, staying for a couple of nights. We talk a little, but mostly we sit and let time pass by between us – a book, a newspaper or a laptop to hand. But we are there together, in that strange twilight moment, and I'm glad of his company.

It's a fortnight after losing Dad that we get another call. Roy's uncle has been killed in a road accident while out cycling. He was the same age as my dad. Then, shortly after this, we hear of the death of a family friend – a gentle soul who'd shown us great kindness over the years.

Death seems to be stalking us and I feel an almost constant anxiety that isn't easily shaken. Now more than ever do I need my garden, nature and the countryside around me. Perhaps with all this death, it's natural to seek out life. I can lose myself in the garden, trimming back, digging up and planting out. I can potter in the warm sanctuary of the greenhouse, seeking out ripe tomatoes and peppers. I can immerse my hands in the soil. And I can walk, crossing fields, leaning on gates, gazing up into the endless blue sky. All these things help, but they can't switch my feelings off completely and neither should I aim for that, for feelings show that we're alive.

I'm asked to housesit Pink Thatch and I willingly accept for a few days, feeling the need to just be me in a home that isn't mine. A change, I think, may help, and it does. I walk their dog around the meadow, I feed the hens and I water the garden and polytunnel, picking fresh salad each day, and I write a little too. I walk around a big field nearby and see nobody else. There is plenty of headspace here; few words are needed. It's the perfect refuge.

My father's funeral is on a bleak day in September. It's raining and the road to the crematorium is dark and glossy. Everyone is huddled under umbrellas and I feel glad to have this extra shield between me and the world. I am with Roy and my brother – my two stalwarts who flank me. My brother and I are giving eulogies and I wonder now at the wisdom of our decision to do this. But we get through it. I am first up because I know I won't be able to speak after hearing my brother. When my moment is over, he stands up and hugs me before taking his place to give his own eulogy.

It all feels too soon, too sudden. I'm not ready to be playing this part in my life yet. I thought there were years more of Dad in our lives, but here we are, at this awful day.

He's gone.

It's just a month after my father's funeral when we hear that our beloved friend Ellie, who's fought a brain tumour valiantly for over five years, has declined further treatment, choosing to spend her last few months at home. It is heartbreaking news and a day we've all been dreading. I suppose I was always carrying that kernel of hope for her full recovery because she had overcome so many obstacles, including two operations and countless bouts of chemotherapy. She so deserved to beat the odds and survive and I'm furious that she's not going to be spared.

I'm finding it difficult to work. Perhaps it's because we've just had a trip to Norwich to see the solicitor and deal with some other business, or perhaps it's because the autumn sun feels more like summer and it's beckoning me outside. I heed its call and leave my desk. The words aren't coming anyway so there's no point labouring at the blank screen.

I find that I'm using myself, measuring myself, analysing how I'm feeling. It adds an odd level of pressure to what I'm going through as I constantly examine it. Am I mining myself for material for a future book, I wonder? Can I use these emotions for a character one day? It's sometimes very odd being a writer. So often, you feel like an outsider, an observer and that can very often shield you a little from life because you're never really in the thick of it – there will always be that little piece of you left outside of any given situation – a piece that's watching carefully and taking notes.

Will a walk make me feel better? How many characters have I sent off on walks in my novels when they have problems to solve? Will my own prescription work for me now? I decide to find out and grab the little bag I take when I go walking. It's a small over-the-shoulder number – just big enough for a bottle of water, my phone, foraging tin, and a notebook and pen in case inspiration strikes.

There's a wonderful Latin phrase which Ronald Blythe taught me: *solvitur ambulando* which means to work it out by walking. I love that so I leave our cottage and walk down the road.

A delivery van pulls up at a house I pass and a man gets out.

'How are you?' he calls cheerily.

You don't want to know, I think but, of course, I don't say that. Instead, I smile while feeling the tears welling up inside me. The slightest thing seems to be setting me off today. My emotions are so close to the surface.

I turn down a little lane. Very few cars come this way and, if they do, it means pushing yourself into the brambly hedge. As the year progresses, the brambles threaten to swallow the lane whole and delight in scratching down the sides of cars which dare to drive its length. But it's quiet today and I have the lane to myself.

There's a favourite oak tree ahead of me and I try and focus on it, but the angst of the past is assaulting me again. I gaze at the tree and make a pact with myself. Once I walk past the tree, I will think only happy thoughts. No past. No future. Just the present moment, I determine. I will focus on the countryside around me. I am ready for nature to cure me, but I can't help wondering if it really has that power. Can the wind blow my grief away? Can rain wash it from me? Can the sun burn it out of me?

I climb over a rickety stile and I'm by the river that slices through the valley. Skeins of cobweb pirouette through the air, catching the sun like spun gold. I collect them on my arms like Thomas Hardy's Tess in that wonderful passage when she's walking through a Dorset dawn.

I force my steps to slow. What can I see? What can I hear? I spy a buzzard high up in the sky and I spot a ladybird under a hazel leaf. I smile. Is this a happy moment or a sad one? Sometimes, it's hard to tell because great beauty can inspire sorrow as you're aware that beauty fades. You're in this moment, really in it, but you're also aware that it's fleeting and you'll never get it back. You'll never be here as you are in this precise moment ever again.

I spy some pineapple weed on the track alongside one of the large fields. It's late in the season but I give them a pinch and find them firm. I might be able to gather enough for a cup of tea or two. I reach into my bag for the small round tin inside for such foraged treats. Finding something like this is rather like winning a prize.

Autumn is a magical time, full of colour, and I love the rusts and russets, the ambers and ochres, the warmth of the air and the blue of the sky that could almost trick you into believing that it's still summer. But summer is long over; the season has changed. Time is moving on.

The Second Spring

During the winter months, there is still plenty to do in the garden. We are plagued by moles who quickly leave over sixty molehills across four separate areas of the garden. We get to work clearing them. Some of the earth they've pushed up through the lawn near the greenhouse is poor and stony while, in the apple tree garden, the earth is dark and loamy and we place it on the no-dig beds, grateful to have this rich addition for growing in come the spring. So the moles are useful for something, at least.

There are endless saplings and bramble bushes to cut back and dig out. It seems like a never-ending task, but it's really quite pleasant, mindful work when the weather is mild. There are also paths of fallen leaves to clear. But I'm leaving them in some of the borders for the protection of the new shoots coming up, and also as a natural organic manure. This is a gift straight from nature after all.

I'm so glad when February finally arrives. Although the wintry weather is far from over, February means that seed sowing can begin – cautiously at first for the days are still cold and daylight hours are short. But I need to start tomatoes, peppers and aubergines if I want a good harvest of their fruit. They need all the days of summer we can give them.

Up until now, I've never really organised my seeds. I've just plonked the packets into tins. Then, as the years passed and I began to develop as a gardener, sowing more seed each year, things began to get out of hand and the one tin of seeds became three. And then I saw the best tip ever – to organise your seeds into the months you're going to be sowing them. Why on earth hadn't I done this before? It seems crazy to me now. I used to just dive in day by day, pulling out a few packets I fancied sowing. It was very hit and miss and seeds were often overlooked.

I have inherited a beautiful old suitcase from my father and it seemed to be begging for a use so Roy made some dividers for it and I now have my fruit and veg seeds on one side and my flowers and herbs on the other. And all are divided neatly by month.

Thinking of the year ahead fills me with optimism and gives me great pleasure and I find myself remembering the highlights of the previous year. The sunflowers peeping over the fence at the front of the cottage are a definite must-repeat. I can't now imagine life without these golden giants. A neighbour has asked if we'll be growing the white cosmos in the front garden again. She tells us that she loved it. It's so rewarding having this sort of feedback and knowing that what you've planted has given joy not only to you but to others. It makes me remember the gardens I've enjoyed over the years. There was a house at Coniston Cold on the A65 in Yorkshire which was famous for its summer display of geraniums. The brilliant reds, yellows and pinks were a joy to behold as you crossed the county on this busy main road. Then there was a garden in the Ruislip suburbs I used to always look out for as the dahlia display was wondrous. Our previous village here in Suffolk had a dahlia-loving gardener too and I always took time to admire the blooms which peeped over the garden wall.

And that's what I want our garden to be for others – something to look forward to. The kind of place where someone slows the car down so that they can take a look. A landmark of loveliness if you will.

Cornflowers are a must for me each year. I love to grow the 'polka dot' variety which not only has blue but pink and purple flowers. They look so jolly grown in terracotta pots which you can place around the garden to cheer up a little corner or to have beside a bench. I have saved lots of seed from last year and this is something I want to do more of. There are few things more gratifying than growing free flowers.

Zinnias have also become a regular feature in our garden. I wasn't sure I'd like these boldly-coloured beauties. They've always looked much too exotic to me but, the first year I grew them, I knew I was hooked. I adored the conical centres and they made the cheeriest of cut flowers for bringing into the house. I discovered that their vase life was very good too.

Snapdragons – antirrhinums – are also a must-have flower. They're annuals but, last year, the plants looked so healthy throughout the winter that I didn't have the heart to lift them and I was rewarded by early spring flowers to cut for the house.

The cold, dark days continue and I'm feeling very glum. I've been hiding away inside, taking few walks, concentrating on the one thing I can control – my writing. I do my best work during the winter months, squirrelling myself away, putting in the hours, getting the words down. I don't mind working hard when the daylight hours are short and I can't get out into the garden, but I miss it so much.

That's why I like to take time off in the summer. And when I say time off, I mean writing in the garden! But I don't like to put any pressure on myself during the golden months of the year. I will often choose a shorter project to tackle like a memoir or novella or – more recently – a screenplay. Novel writing takes time and patience. It's a huge commitment both physically and mentally, and the summer months aren't for that.

We have two named storms in February and some brutally cold weather during March then, suddenly, the sun appears and I race out into the garden.

I'm in the hen run when I hear skylarks – they are dancing in the air above me. So close! I've never seen a pair together so low in the sky before. Spring really feels as if it's arrived and I breathe in the clear air.

There are violets in the lawn and around the base of our old apple tree, joining the snowdrops and the early daffodils. And the first yellow blooms of my wallflowers in pots are peeping out. I can't wait to see them in full flower. I saw a row of them last spring when on a walk in a neighbouring village. They were jostled together in russet and golden loveliness beside a beautiful old brick wall outside a converted schoolhouse. It was like a scene from a Miss Read novel and I knew I had to grow some.

Tulips and alliums are peeping out of the borders in the front garden. I remember the warm autumn days when I planted them, my knees in the grass, bending forward in to my circular borders. I have chosen two pink tulip beauties: Angelique, which I'm trying again after previously failing with them, and Finola, and I'm not disappointed when their pastel petals open. They are gloriously feminine. But now comes the dilemma – I'm desperate to cut some for the house, but they look so wonderful in the garden. If I cut just a few, I can have fun arranging them, choosing a vase and a place to put them. I can photograph them too and, that way, they will live forever. This is my internal dialogue as I grab the secateurs.

Roy has spent two entire days up in the apple tree, cutting water sprouts – the long thin shoots that sap away so much of a tree's energy while rarely producing any fruit. I make a start clearing the branches away. It's pleasant work, to begin with, my back soon feeling the familiar ache of gardening which has been forgotten during the long winter months. I needed this day in the garden. After spending so many months cocooned indoors, living in my head, writing, it's felt good to spend the entire day outside doing something physical and making a visible difference to our environment.

March, April and May

A brilliantly bright March day dawns. It's a few days since the funeral of my friend Ellie, and I can't pretend it's been an easy time. But the funeral – like her – was beautiful, unique and quirky, taking place outdoors on her beloved farm in the Stour Valley. There was music, poetry and the song of skylarks above us. It's so hard to imagine a world without her in it. She will be missed by so many of us. I can't believe that there'll be no more fun trips with her to see churches and museums, art galleries or windswept beaches. Ellie was one of life's truly brilliant people. We always had a good time when we saw her. Laughter came easily – even when she was in the middle of chemotherapy. I remember one time when we were going out somewhere and she was sitting in the back of our car.

'Oh, dear – my hair's just fallen out!' she said, matter-of-factly.

I flinched, not knowing how to respond to such a frightening declaration, but Ellie handled it beautifully.

'I'll save it for the birds to make nests with,' she said, stuffing the hair into her capacious handbag. It's a moment I'll never forget because it encapsulates her spirit so perfectly.

Phoebe, our Black Orpington hen, isn't in the hen run. Can she be laying an egg? She hasn't for over a year, but maybe she's feeling the surge of spring? I open the coop door and peer inside. She isn't laying an egg; she's not well. We isolate her and ring the vet and Roy goes to fetch the medication that's been prescribed.

There are no end of things I should be doing as far as work and housework are concerned, but the blue sky and sunshine are calling me and I need some time out with everything that's happened recently. Sometimes, you have to ask yourself, what would you benefit most from today? Rarely is the answer: working more. So my boots go on and I take off. I'm not going far – just along the country lanes and down by the little river near us. I might spot a kingfisher.

The Alexanders are flowering in the lanes already and the promise of some free food is exciting. Our own calabrese planted last year is beginning to bolt so the Alexanders are timely indeed. Their scent in the sun is heady.

There is a skylark showering its song upon me in a bliss of bright notes. I'm immediately reminded of Ellie's funeral and how these gentle birds' music brought us so much solace. But how hard it is to hear them on this beautiful spring day that Ellie isn't here to see.

Alas, Phoebe's health declines quickly and we are forced to make that toughest of decisions and have her put to sleep. Her dark, glossy presence will be missed in the garden and it's particularly hard to lose her after already losing Portia and Mini P just a few months ago. Our flock is much depleted and it makes me sad.

One morning, I see a goldfinch sitting at the very top of a long blossom-covered branch in one of our cherry trees. It's a windy day and the little bird is swaying to and fro as if he's on some kind of fairground ride yet, all the time, he is singing. And it's such a wonderful song. It's as if he's proclaiming to the world that nothing will stop him from singing. It might be blowing a gale, but it is spring and he has a song to sing. I love that.

As always, there is plenty to do in the garden. Sometimes, I'll make a quick list of chores I need to tackle and, on a good day, I'll get them done. But there are also days when I go out – fully intending to do certain jobs – but then spot something else that needs my attention: some deadheading, perhaps, or a plant that suddenly needs staking or another that needs to be potted up. The best days are the ones when there is no list whatsoever, but the sun entices me outside and I simply potter, moving around the garden, noting what needs my attention. Those, I think, are the happiest gardening days.

April brings us a real treat. Back in our Mulberry Cottage days, one of our good friends emailed me to tell me about Yalda Davis – a cellist who is on a very special mission to play in all of Suffolk's medieval churches, raising money for Suffolk Historic Churches Trust as she goes. Old buildings and beautiful music are two of my favourite things and I quickly found her on Instagram and saw that she lived in a thatched farmhouse with a garden full of animals. This was my kind of person, I thought, and I sent her a quick message. It wasn't long before we met up. She visited us at Old Thatch during our first summer and we visited her at Crossways Farm – a delightful pink Grade II thatched paradise of a place tucked down a quiet country lane.

We met her two rabbits who live in the front room where they roam around freely and we're introduced to her pet degu – a gerbil-like animal who might be small but who has a huge personality. I instantly fell in love when he held his front leg up to be tickled underneath it.

We had tea and cake in the farmhouse kitchen which is full of beautiful handmade pottery mugs, bowls and plates. An enormous window overlooks a garden and I couldn't wait to explore. Yalda took us outside to meet the

hens, and then her pair of goats which she let out to trot behind us as we walked around the garden, crossing the bridge with us over the pond and playfully headbutting us for attention as we admired the trees.

Crossways Farm is the kind of place that's hard to leave. There's just so much joy and beauty there, and a real sense of peace.

In April, we get a very special invitation to visit again and the garden is full of bright daffodils. Yalda is hosting a small, private concert in her front room. She will be playing the cello, accompanied by a pianist friend. Her sister, also a musician, is there too, on page-turning duty for the pianist. It is a delightful afternoon. First, there are refreshments in the kitchen where we chat to the other guests and then we're ushered through to the living room. Yalda warns us that the rabbits are free-ranging and to take care when moving chairs.

There's a moment when one movement of music finishes and Yalda excuses herself. It seems that Ilo the goat has jumped a fence onto the terrace and has to be returned to the garden. This causes much hilarity. It's certainly something that audiences at regular concerts wouldn't have the pleasure of witnessing.

As the musicians play on, I look around the ancient room I'm sitting in. The music is drifting over me and one of the rabbits is sitting contentedly nearby, and I can't help but smile. Moments like this in life are so very precious and should be cherished. Yalda has created something so very special at Crossways Farm and I'm overwhelmed by her kindness in sharing her home and her passion for her music.

We have had a very dry spring. There have been no April showers and it's the fourth of May when we get the first rain in weeks. It is very welcome, helping to replenish the empty water butts.

In the evening, I walk into the valley. Everything feels cool and fresh. I see a deer and stand still, watching as he runs across the field. I wish I could describe the way he runs more poetically. 'Runs' seems such an ordinary word for such a balletic movement. In the Ted Hughes poem *Roe Deer*, he describes the animals as 'riding their legs' which I feel is close to succeeding in capturing their fairground-like movement. The deer crosses into an adjacent field and gives a loud bark. Is that aimed at me? There is a pheasant honking somewhere too. I am a trespasser here – a twilight interloper who isn't welcome in this place at this time of night. But I needed this evening walk.

I listen to my body more these days and ask what I need most: A walk? A swim? A rest? Sometimes, I'll start a walk with a knot in my stomach and it will take a while to shake the spectre of grief from my spirit. Then, somewhere between watching the poppies dance and noticing the first elderflowers bloom, the knot loosens a little.

By the end of May, the countryside looks so different. The cow parsley is already past its best, forming seed heads, so the footpaths have lost a little of their froth. Nettles take its place, soaring up to sting an unwary walker. A few scarlet poppies dot themselves in the wheat field which seems tinged pink in the evening light as I walk out to watch the sunset.

There is wild rocket growing by the river – pale pink and white. Campions mirror it with their own pretty flowers. This is a favourite part of my walk, in the heart of the valley by the little river that wends through this part of the county. There are two mother cows with their calves in one of the fields here now, their warm, animal smell heavy on the evening air.

I notice the golden drifts of buttercups in the next field and then my attention comes back to the path I'm walking on, my legs brushing through the long grasses and the air filled with ghostly moths.

Of course, there are dozens of plants and flowers around me which I cannot name and it frustrates me not knowing what they are. But it doesn't really matter. I can still enjoy their beauty. You don't need to name a thing to appreciate it.

Abundance

Once again, the greenhouse tells me I've sown too many seeds. It's that awkward period in May when the tender perennials like dahlias and agapanthus are still sheltering under glass and the annuals like cosmos, snapdragons, zinnias and squashes can't yet be planted out until we're certain the last frost has been. Meanwhile, the tomatoes, aubergines and peppers are growing apace, demanding to be potted up. There is standing room only now and I'm constantly shifting pots and trays, trying to give everything the attention it needs. I can't wait for the longer, warmer days when I can start planting out.

I try not to get stressed by how much I have to do, but I can virtually hear the plants screaming at me. There are two full trays of celery plants as well as a smaller one chockfull of seedlings. I had no idea all these seeds would germinate and I certainly can't plant them all. There simply isn't room for seventy-plus celery plants. I decide to give some away.

When the garden workload seems overwhelming, I ask myself, what do I *most* need to do today? I look around. Which plants are drying out or yellowing and need potting up or planting out *the most*? But, equally important, I find, is to ask myself what do *I* need the most from the garden today? The two might not always tally.

It's the same with the beautiful red nicotiana (tobacco plant) seeds I collected from the garden. I'd never grown this kind before and liberally sprinkled seed in a tray. It is now groaning with life. My densely-sown salad trays are easier to deal with and I start planting these out in the garden. I rarely direct sow salad as the seedlings are so vulnerable to slugs and snails. I like to start them in trays or tubs and watch as the seedlings develop into healthy little plants. I then separate them and plant them individually around the garden, in raised beds or in the no-dig beds.

Once the last frost is over, I begin to plant out the flowers I've grown from seed. I have three trays of ammi majus – Queen Anne's Lace. It is a glorious, wafty flower that looks like a slightly more elegant cow parsley. This year, I am going to plant some of it with cosmos Purity and I can't wait to see the result. It should be a very pretty pairing. As I plant the seedlings into the circular bed at the back of our cottage, I notice the date I marked on the plant label. It tells me that I saved the seeds in the middle of

February. On this warm, sunny day, it's hard to imagine that cold one three months ago. And in another three months, these little plants will have reached maturity and probably be taller than me.

We widen a couple of the no-dig beds we made last year and make one huge one in the front garden. The space here can take it and still leaves plenty of lawn. I'm calling this new bed the pumpkin patch and promptly plant around twenty squashes in it. Once the job is done, I sit down and stare at it in wonder, thinking to myself that the area it takes up is the same size as my entire yard when I was renting my ground-floor flat in the late nineties in Yorkshire. It almost makes me feel I'm greedy to have so much space here at Old Thatch, but I did wait a long time for it, I tell myself, and it couldn't have a more appreciative owner.

One May morning, I walk out into the garden with Hattie by my side. She usually takes off, running across the meadow in easy strides to stick her head under the hedge and see what's going on there but, today, she looks at me with an expression I understand all too well. It's too warm to run, she says. It's too warm to work, I reply. She walks by my side, looking up at me attentively. She knows where we're going.

A moment later, I sit down on the sloping bit of grass which looks over the back of the cottage. Hattie is delighted. She loves sitting on the grass next to me, pushing her body against mine. It feels good just to sit, my arm around her, the two of us gazing into the garden and up at the blue sky, taking it all in. Sometimes, we'll sit on a bench. Since she was a puppy, I've encouraged Hattie to jump up onto the garden benches to sit beside me and she'll often run ahead of me to get to them. Then we sit in companionable silence, her soft panting the only noise. It's the kind of warm sunny day when the Famous Five would have jumped on their bikes and cycled towards the nearest adventure, but we're contented to just sit and stare into the depths of the garden, dreaming the day away.

One warm evening, Roy and I, along with Hattie, visit a local bluebell wood. On the way, we pass the old converted school house with a marvellously mellowed brick wall in front of which grow the red and yellow wallflowers which inspired me to grow our own. I stop to inhale their musky sweetness.

We leave the lane and head along a footpath that dips into the wood and there they are. The bluebells. We stop to photograph them and inhale that magical perfume. But the scent of bluebells is soon overtaken by the overpowering smell of wild garlic and yet we can't see it. We walk on, going ever downhill until we spy it at the valley bottom. It's the largest expanse of wild garlic I've ever seen and the smell is deep and strong – a savoury

counterpart to the sweetness of the bluebells. Our olfactory senses are being overwhelmed; it's almost too much. But this is one of the joys of late spring and I know we'll never stop seeking it out.

I love the late light evenings of May. It's nine o'clock, the hens have just gone in and I've finally come inside after a whole day in the garden. It's been blissful – sowing seeds, potting up and planting out. We also ate a fair amount of home-grown produce too in a pesto that included basil, marjoram, Jack by the Hedge, spinach, mint and sage. A totally delicious day!

Another evening, I'm sitting under the apple tree drinking fresh mint tea and it strikes me that I'm in the garden, *drinking* the garden.

May continues to delight. I'm walking home one evening through the fields when I see the distinctive black and white stripy head of a badger peeping out from its sett on a little hill. I gasp and freeze, hoping he hasn't spotted me, but he disappears into his hole. But, to my great joy, there's another and I watch as he trots across the field.

The next evening, I return with Roy, hoping we'll get lucky and spot the badgers. We see movement in a little wood and watch as two or three youngsters dart around the undergrowth. It's hard to see them; we only catch glimpses of a nose, back or tail. But it's enough. We can hear their funny little grunts too. And they seem to be playing or grooming. I wish we had a better view, but what a privilege it is to share this space with them for a while, and it's wonderful to be out in this beautiful place in the evening, the hawthorn thick with its white blossom, the great oak tree resplendent with its spring foliage. Twice, we spy a fox crossing the field, and we see lots of roe deer too, racing across the space to safety, barking in annoyance at our presence.

Climbing over the stile, we walk up the lane back to our cottage. The sky is darkening and a bat flies overhead. I love being out at this time. It's so quiet and still. It's hard to be indoors on such evenings and I prolong the day by walking around the garden, taking in the plants and flowers at dusk.

Suffolk Friends

June is a wonderful time as artists across the county open their studios to the public. Each year, Roy and I choose a few to visit and it's always exciting to meet new artists, admire their work and see their studios. You never quite know what you're going to discover and we've made some lovely friends through the scheme.

June also means more visits to open gardens and Jane from our village accompanies me to one across the border in Essex. When we arrive, parking in a field overlooking a beautiful valley, we see a young woman at the entrance ready to take our entry fee. She's sitting in an open horsebox – her makeshift office for the day.

Alas, it isn't a glorious summer's day and we shelter under umbrellas as we walk around the grounds, but it is still wonderful to be outside admiring somebody else's hard work and this garden is a bit special. The large country manor house is set in a valley next to a church. It feels wonderfully rural despite being just a stone's throw from the city of Colchester.

There are deep borders full of pink roses and alliums, and the trees are astonishing. There is a particularly impressive ginkgo – the largest outside of Kew, we read, and a beautiful cedar tree too.

We walk around the little lake, the rain dimpling the dark surface, the irises doing their best to bring a little colour to the wet day. We then head to the delightful walled garden with a lean-to greenhouse and borders full of peonies on the verge of blooming. Along one of the walls, tall irises in purples, pinks and yellows brighten the scene.

We stop by the plant stall which has been set up by a local grower and I'm delighted to discover so many plants which I am already growing, having sown the seeds earlier in the year. I recognise most of them and realise how much I've learned over the years, just picking things up as I go along. Learning through love of the subject – isn't that always the best way?

There is tea and cake available in the church next door. We leave our wet umbrellas in the porch and queue inside. The weather hasn't put anyone off from enjoying a day out and we are soon at the front of the queue choosing our cake. I have to say that I am a chocolate cake sort of a girl, but there is also coffee and walnut on offer. This is a great temptation as I know in my heart of hearts that I will probably never make it myself – not being a coffee drinker. Jane plumps for the coffee and I do too. The young girl serving cuts Jane a perfect slice, but she seems to be struggling with mine.

'I'm making a mess of this one,' she tells me and I watch as the pretty frosting is squashed and splatted onto my plate. Of course, being English, I just smile and don't complain. It will all taste the same, I think to myself as we make our way to a pew.

It feels very odd to be sitting in a church beside ancient tombs, rhapsodising over cake. But everyone seems to think it perfectly normal. I tell Jane that Roy and I have been invited to a wedding and the invite encourages vintage clothes to be worn. This is exciting because I am lucky enough to own three dresses worn by the actress Juliette Binoche in the film *Chocolat*, set in the 1950s. When Roy and I were living in London, an auction of clothes from film and TV came up at Bonhams and I couldn't resist going along – just to look, you understand. Well, one thing led to another and I got carried along in the excitement of everything and, as a lifelong fan of La Binoche, I couldn't resist a bid. Of course, Roy found out how naughty I'd been before I had a chance to tell him myself because the BBC news cameras were there and just happened to film the very moment when my paddle rose to make my winning bid!

I tell Jane about the dresses and that I'm going to attempt to make some kind of fascinator or flower ornament for my hair. This is when she mentions Annie. We met Annie soon after we moved into Old Thatch. She's lived in the village for fifty years and remembers when our cottage was two separate homes.

'You need to see her,' Jane tells me. 'She has hats.'

'Hats?'

'In a shed in her garden. She was going into business but lost her partner. I'm sure she'd have something suitable.'

Well, before I have a chance to call round, something amusing happens. I'm digging up ground elder in the front garden, my hair squashed under a cap, my nails full of dirt, when a car pulls up. It's Annie.

'Jane tells me you'd like a hat for a wedding.'

My mouth breaks into a smile. Word gets around fast in a small village.

'Come on round,' she tells me and I run inside to clean my gardener's nails and make myself look worthy of a wedding hat.

I walk round the side of her neat bungalow. The garden is a little paradise full of huge opium poppies. The shed is open for me and we venture inside. The hats are all shrouded in white tissue paper, floating on the shelves like little coloured ghosts, and I can't wait to see them revealed. Annie has placed a mirror near the door and we begin our search, starting with a pink fascinator covered in little felt violets. It has a tiny net you wear over your face and it sparkles with sequins. I put it on and gasp. It's perfect and it will go with the pink dress I've chosen. Annie agrees and I panic for a moment, thinking that she won't let me try on any of the other hidden beauties. But I needn't have worried because she seems as keen as I am to have a little dressing-up session. So we continue.

There's a huge black and beige hat that reminds us both of Audrey Hepburn. There's a sky-blue hat which is all froth. I call it 'The Cloud' and immediately want to take it home. And there are scarlet hats, midnight-blue hats, gold hats and green. I wish I had more heads so that I could wear them all.

'Do you like brooches?' she suddenly asks me.

'I love brooches!' I exclaim and quickly tell her about the heroine in my new trilogy who is designing a range of brooches because I've always been obsessed with them. I've been wearing them since I was a teenager, aware that they've always been deemed old-fashioned. But I love them. What I don't tell Annie is there's scene in my trilogy where the heroine, Abi, is given a brooch by a retired friend. The coincidence is not lost on me. It's one of those strange moments where it feels like I've written a scene in my own life by creating a fictional one first.

Annie disappears into the house, leaving me alone with the hats. I can't resist uncovering a few more, trying on a green and black creation that reminds me of a chocolate lime. It would be perfect with one of the other Juliette Binoche dresses I have, but I've chosen to wear the pink one.

When Annie returns, she teases me. 'Been enjoying the hats?'

'Oh, yes!'

She opens her right hand and I gasp at the sight of four beautiful brooches – all vintage. One is a midnight-blue round brooch featuring an eighteenth-century couple depicted in gold. It's Limoges. There are two pretty flower brooches with lovely old clasps and I can see them looking very sweet on summer hats. And the last is a show-stopping diamante number which the magpie in me adores.

'I don't wear them,' Annie says, 'and it's a shame that they're not enjoyed.'

I thank her and assure her that they will be worn and treasured.

I walk the short distance back to our cottage, wearing a straw hat decorated with tiny pink rose buds and holding two huge bags of hats, one in either hand. It feels extraordinary to have had this experience right in the middle of our tiny village.

Once home, I treat Roy to a little fashion show, enjoying his expression at some of the hats. And I find one of my own favourite everyday hats and place one of Annie's flower brooches on it. The colours blend perfectly. It's as if the hat and the brooch were destined to meet.

The only thing about being invited to a wedding is that I have to take care of my hands and nails. I'm a terrible one for gardening without wearing gloves. I know I should wear them more to protect myself, but I very often just step outside, spot a couple of weeds and think, 'I'll just pull those two up.' Of course, before I know it, I'm elbow deep in weeding and, invariably, my hands will soon discover a thistle, nettle or bramble. It's a painful lesson I really should have learned by now.

The other thing I'm prone to is deadheading with my right thumbnail. It's a hard habit to break as I'm walking round the garden and the state of my thumbnail is really quite shocking. So, in the run-up to the wedding, I stop deadheading or at least I make sure I use secateurs and pop on a pair of gardening gloves for good measure.

Kerrie and Emilie's wedding is glorious. The ceremony is outdoors up in the hills of Norwich. I wear my Juliette Binoche dress and the gorgeous floral-festooned fascinator Annie has gifted me. The day is full of music, colour and love.

Coming home, I get changed and walk around the garden checking on everything. The light is fading from the sky and the hens have gone to bed.

I walk past a rose bush and automatically reach out to deadhead it, smiling to myself as I do so. With the wedding now over, I've got my thumb back.

One of the perks of living in our village is that so many of our neighbours are keen gardeners and it's very easy to fall into a conversation about what's growing well and what isn't. Like the weather, it seems to be a favourite subject. One afternoon, I'm planting out some cosmos in the front garden, having cleared yet more ground elder from the border first, when neighbours pass by. It's Simon and Julie from across the road, out for a walk with their dog. I tell them what I've been up to garden-wise and how I recently lost three newly-planted rows of ammi majus and that I'd seen a baby rabbit in the garden as well as a young hare. Simon nods. He's got the elusive black rabbits in his garden. I've seen them in the valley. They're rather special, but you still wouldn't want to find them in the garden nibbling. The older I get, the more sympathy I have with Beatrix Potter's Mr McGregor.

Simon and Julie admire the little plant stall I have by the gate and it isn't long before we're arranging a plant swap. I offer them some of my excess celery while Julie admires my hollyhocks and I remember that I have a spare tray of seedlings. I say I've been admiring their pink valerian and Julie promises me some.

The next day, I deliver a tray of celery, another of hollyhocks and a pot of young red nicotiana. A couple of days later, Simon walks round wielding a wheelbarrow. It's a wonderful sight and makes me smile. Plants bring so much joy and sharing that joy with others is a wonderful thing.

Simon's barrow contains the valerian, a couple of house plant cuttings and a beautiful shrub called a leycesteria that I've never come across before. He warns me that it will get as tall as he is, and then shows me a photo of it on his phone. He tells me of its beautiful deep purple flowers and berries as I unload the plants. I will think carefully before deciding where to plant it but welcome it to our cottage garden.

As he bumps the wheelbarrow down the path to leave, I open the front gate for him and tell him to take one of the pitcher plants from my stall – no charge. We are gardening buddies now.

I take great pleasure in sharing the bounty we have. As I've already confessed, I oversow and end up with too many plants and there's nothing lovelier than handing a potted tomato to a neighbour or a visitor, or taking a pretty geranium cutting to a friend's house. If you allow yourself the time to sow seeds, take cuttings or divide your plants, you will always have something to give away or swap with a friend or neighbour.

Summer Blooms

It's the middle of June and it's really warming up. I get out into the garden as early as I can to water the greenhouse and luxuriate in the warm aroma of things growing. We have young tomatoes now. It will be a while yet until we can pick them for eating, but how I long to see that first glorious red fruit and pop it into my mouth while it's still sun-warmed.

The cherries are ripening, but they're falling as they do, or are being plundered by flocks of starlings who are taking them no matter how unripe and small they are. We must net some if we are to get any at all.

One warm morning, I begin replenishing my terracotta pots. I've been a very bad custodian of them, expecting the displays to flourish through years of neglect, but I make amends now, loosening the edges and carefully tipping the contents of each pot out, weeding out the interlopers of which there are quite a few. I discover a few young cotoneasters from Mulberry Cottage. They must have germinated from berries dropped into the pot. My instinct is to pop them onto the compost heap, but then I remember how much the wild birds loved feasting on the berries and so I pot them up, determining to find a home for them somewhere at Old Thatch.

This pot I'm liberating contains a once beautiful butterfly lavender, but it's swamped by dandelions, self-seeded marjoram and the cotoneaster. As soon as it's freed, I trim some of the dead wood. It's a gangly thing, but the blooms are still lovely so I give it a chance with some fresh compost, planting a few Sweet Williams for company and some snapdragons for instant summer colour.

As I return the replenished pots to the front doorstep, I admire the river of foxgloves growing around the cottage. They are nestled under the wisteria and are mostly dark pink, but there are a few white ones which are lovely, their flowers wonderfully speckled. There is a craze for a foxglove called Sutton's Apricot and I have to say that it is particularly beautiful. It's funny the way that certain flowers come in and out of fashion. I think it's all rather silly. If you like a flower, you should have it in your garden whether it's in vogue or not. Dahlias were deeply unpopular for a few years, but have now made a huge comeback. There's one – rather like the apricot foxglove – that has been particularly popular: Cafe au Lait. For the last few autumns, it has dominated Instagram, its enormous, petal-filled head popping up

everywhere. Of course, I had to have one. It was just too impressive not to have in the garden and it's been a delightful addition to floral displays when brought inside. You just don't have to mind a few earwigs!

Now, the flower of the moment seems to be the poppy 'Patty's Plum' – a fabulous oriental poppy in a rich purple. It looks like glossy tissue paper and I think we have it here at Old Thatch. We are certainly lucky to have many oriental poppies which self-seed around the paved areas, in beds and in the gravel path at the front of the cottage. There's something very special about the delicacy of a poppy – their stems seem so vigorous and strong and yet their petals are so fragile and fleeting. I love the way the petals fall confetti-like to the ground, leaving the patterned seed head. I leave this on all summer, often photographing them, and allowing the seeds to form in their rattly home so that the plant can self-seed and give its gift of beauty to the world all over again the next year. And the seed heads are also beautiful to dry and display in the house too.

I have always wanted a pink peony – the sort that looks like a ballerina's tutu or a blowsy double rose that's been magnified by at least three. Well, I was lucky enough to discover one already here at Old Thatch. It is a true beauty – its petals the most perfect pale pink, the scent rich and deep. The first year, we didn't stake it properly in time and had a battle on our hands with garden twine. It looked a bit of a mess. But this second year, we're ready, popping in stakes ahead of its blooms. The flowers are large and heavy and have a tendency to droop so staking is essential. Their size also gives me a good excuse to cut a few flowers for the house as it helps to give the plant a little of its bounce back. And what a joy it is to gather an armful of the glorious pink heads, arranging them simply in a crystal vase to place on the dresser. I spend a while photographing the arrangement and then, a few days later, pick more, placing them in a vintage jug together with the scented white blooms of philadelphus and the feathery perfection of fennel. The three together are stunning.

New Faces

For us, summer very often brings a few new faces into the garden. This is the time of year when we take a look at our flock of hens and see how many more we can accommodate. With the sad losses of the last few months, we decide to find three new gorgeous girls and soon discover a local company. We're going to choose some beautiful hybrid point of lay hens as we already have four ex-bat girls and I fear not being able to tell them all apart if we get more, but I have to admit to feeling slightly guilty about not rehoming more ex-bats. Next time, I promise myself.

We look at the different breeds on offer on the company's website and draw up a shortlist. We don't want to be too prescriptive, though, as it's always fun to look on the day and see the different personalities.

With two boxes made up for travel, we head across the county to meet our new companions. It's always one of my favourite days and I'm bubbling with excitement. We choose a beautiful Light Sussex hybrid, a golden girl, and a gorgeous Legbar-type with a little pom-pom head who will lay us blue-green eggs. I name the white hen Rose, the golden girl Topaz, and the pom-pom girl will be Blossom – names from Dodie Smith's *I Capture the Castle* – a gorgeous, coming-of-age book set here in Suffolk.

We take them home and get them settled. The old girls show an immediate interest, but there aren't any obvious protests as there sometimes are. We've divided the run in two, giving the new girls both privacy and isolation so we can monitor the health of the birds before integrating them. And how lovely it is to watch them. Only one puts herself to bed on the first night and Roy and I catch the other two. But, by the third night, they've got used to their new home.

We're impressed with their boldness. They are the cheekiest and most adventurous hens we've ever had. They're so keen to integrate and, despite us clipping their wings, they prove able to leap over the barrier dividing them from the old girls. This isn't ideal and we do our best to keep them separate, but they are great jumpers. I worry that this might prove an issue later on when we let them out to free range. Will they be able to jump over the garden gate to the great world beyond? I hope they quickly learn that this is home and that they won't feel the need to try to escape.

It is less than three weeks after we bring the new girls home that they all start laying eggs, and the funny thing is that they choose the wooden coop in which to lay them rather than the plastic one they've been sleeping in. Perhaps they've seen our established flock climbing the ladder and then sounding the alarm once they've finished their chicken's business.

Blossom is the first to lay. Indeed, we guessed she would be as her comb is much larger than the other two's – a sign of maturity. I'm pottering around in the garden one morning when I hear a strange scratching coming from the coop. None of our girls has ever made such a noise and I go to inspect. It's Blossom, making a little nest for herself. Nature is miraculous and my heart swells with pride as I wonder how she's feeling. This is a big moment for her – her first egg. Is she anxious? Does she know what's happening? She seems to know what to do so I leave her to it and it isn't long before she lays her first perfect pale blue egg.

Over the next few days, she lays a lovely blue egg every day. She's working hard. It's as if she's become quickly addicted to this egg laying lark.

It isn't long before Topaz and Rose join her. Like Blossom, they venture up the ladder into the wooden coop and lay their first eggs on the same day. I'm so proud of my new girls. They are a wonderful addition to the Old Thatch flock.

Floral Ambitions

I've always loved how writers are also, very often, passionate gardeners. The two loves seem to go hand in hand quite naturally and both, I feel, require similar traits. For instance, I think all writers and gardeners are natural optimists. A writer will start out with a tiny seed of an idea, hoping it will germinate and become a full blown story given enough time and energy. Likewise, gardeners sow and plant, trusting that the energy they invest will result in something beautiful – or edible!

Writers and gardeners aren't afraid to dedicate great swathes of time to their passion. Nothing is quick or easy. You cannot write a novel or create a garden in a single day or even a season. And you need to be able to plan although I have to admit that I tend to plough right in with both my writing and gardening, planning very little. I like to think that I'm an instinctive storyteller. It's pretty much the same in the garden for me – I know roughly what I want, but I rarely draw diagrams or measure anything. That would seem much too much like work, and gardening is more akin to play for me. It's my time off, my joy, my release. Tape measures and plans have no place there.

I don't think of myself as a patient person although I guess I must be to be a writer and gardener as neither of those pursuits allow for instant gratification. A novel can take many months if not years from initial inspiration to final publication, and a garden can take multiple years to create. In contrast, a floral display is relatively quick to put together. But the trick is to give yourself time within your day. You have to allow yourself to focus and really enjoy the flowers rather than squeezing your display in between other jobs. That's what I find, at least.

I remember the time I did a pottery course and fully expected to be able to master the potter's wheel and create something beautiful by the end of the day. After all, it looks so easy, doesn't it? I just imagined I'd pick it up, but that would be doing this craft a great disservice. Like any, it takes time, patience and great dedication to create something of beauty. Flower arranging is the same – it's a real art and I've been enjoying learning some of the theory in an online course by the inspirational Willow Crossley, but I try not to put any pressure on myself when creating a display. I know this isn't my main passion like it is for some of the Instagram florists I follow. I don't dedicate the main part of my day to growing, picking, arranging and photographing my flowers. I just want to create something lovely to look at for a few days – to brighten up a corner of our cottage and bring a smile to my face whenever I look at it.

I've long held a fascination for florists. I think it began as a teenager when I had my first Saturday job in a local newsagents. It was always busy with customers ordering magazines, paying for their weekly deliveries of papers, buying cigarettes, sweets and cans of drink. My favourite days – which didn't happen very often – were when I was asked to go and help in the florists next door. It was a world away from the hustle and bustle of the newsagents and I'll never forget the wonderful scent from being surrounded by cut flowers, nor the joy of pulling out a sheet of pretty paper to wrap a bunch up for a smiling customer.

Perhaps this brief encounter with floristry led me to make the heroine of one of my early romantic comedies, *Molly's Millions*, the owner of a flower shop called The Bloom Room. Indeed, the heroine of my latest Christmas novella, *The Wrong Ghost*, is also a florist.

There are some gorgeous books which will tell you all you need to know about growing and arranging flowers and I've listed a few at the end of this book. They go into much more detail than I do if you want to know more. But here's how I go about it.

Flowers should be picked early in the morning or late in the evening when they are hydrated and their stems are at their strongest. Contrary to all the beautiful photographs you see online of people wafting around their gardens with their freshly-cut flowers in a picturesque trug or basket, flowers should be placed into water immediately after cutting or they will quickly wilt. By cutting a flower, you've removed it from its water source so you need to take care of it.

I truly love to give myself a few quiet moments in the garden first thing in the morning, walking around the flower beds and seeing what looks beautiful and thinking about what I can bring together to make a display. I get so much pleasure from choosing a few blooms, particularly if I've grown them myself from seed – that's especially rewarding.

I'm no expert on conditioning flowers, but I'm learning new tricks all the time and have recently started searing my stems once I've brought them indoors. This helps to extend a flower's vase life. You simply boil a kettle, fill a strong jug or mug with the water and pop about ten percent of the stem in the freshly boiled water, being careful to protect the flower heads from the steam. The thicker the stem, the longer you leave it so something like a cosmos might only need five to ten seconds, but a woody lilac stem would benefit for up to half a minute.

Once seared, plunge your flowers into deep, cool water. You can leave them to rest a while before arranging. Somewhere cool and shady, away from direct sunlight, is ideal.

One of my favourite parts of floral arranging is picking a container for the display. I have a little obsession with beautiful vases and jugs and I'm always looking out for them whenever we pop into antiques centres, charity shops or summer fetes. I get so excited when I spot something pretty that other eyes seem to have overlooked. I never spend a fortune on anything and some of my favourites have actually been real bargains. There was a really beautiful jug I spotted at a recent summer fete in a neighbouring village. It was a soft cream colour, a very elegant shape and about twelve inches tall. But it was the flowers that really sold it to me. It was as if it was made for me with its painting of pink roses on the front and exquisite raised detailing. I loved it and quickly decided how much I was willing to pay for it, daring to ask the stallholder a moment later.

'A pound,' she said, almost hesitantly. I tried not to fall over backwards as I quickly picked it up and claimed it as mine.

I have another favourite jug from a small tea set inherited from my grandmother. It's very delicate and I'm always careful when I use it, but it's too pretty to just tuck away in a cupboard. I do think lovely things should be used and enjoyed.

But you don't have to have inherited pieces or spend on vintage jugs. I get just as much pleasure from using a pretty jam jar from the supermarket. There are some gorgeous ones if you look for them. I've also used maple syrup and honey jars and the latest addition to my ever-expanding collection is a tahini jar which I noticed was a particularly delightful shape. I will often tie a ribbon around them and fill them with freshly-cut flowers from the garden as a gift for a friend. You can also use regular kitchen glasses, pretty mugs and even cereal bowls if you have a florist's frog to secure your flowers.

Basically, have fun with your flowers. Don't put any pressure on yourself. Enjoy the blooms, the scent, the colours, and the shapes they create. Flowers are life-enhancing. They ask so little but give so much. It's a privilege to share the planet with them and we should never take them for granted.

One of the things I've learned from my Floral Abundance course in the walled garden and the Willow Crossley course I'm doing is confidence. My creations might not be quite as perfect as I'd like them to be, but I'm far more assured now. One summer's day, I was sitting under the apple tree at my laptop when Roy started pruning a few of the new water sprouts, dropping them onto the ground below. I looked up from my work, cast my eyes down to the discarded branches and immediately saw them as foliage for a display.

I'm looking at the garden through new eyes these days. Nothing is safe from my secateurs now – I have confidence!

The Heatwave

In the depths of winter, I always dream of summer but, when July arrives and the temperature soars, I'm not quite sure how to respond and suddenly hope to look out on a cloudy grey sky when I draw the curtains in the morning.

Temperatures are up to an unprecedented forty degrees Celsius and we hear that a fire broke out at a friend's farm, dangerously close to the farmhouse. Luckily, it was dealt with quickly. Our lawn is yellow and crispy underfoot, making it very unpleasant for bare feet. The greenhouse and garden pots need regular attention and all my new plants are struggling. Young pumpkins are drying and wrinkling on the plants and other squash plants have shrivelled up altogether. It's hard work keeping everything watered sufficiently and I feel like I'm failing. I'm used to watering the greenhouse and garden pots daily in summer but, this year, I need to keep a close eye on all the garden beds and no-dig beds too.

I've planted out so many things and all my young flowers are suffering. The cosmos is a fraction of the height it should be and the sunflowers aren't tall enough to peep over the fence and nod their golden faces at passers-by this year. My snapdragons have developed a horrible disease and have to be pulled up and I'm not sure what's happened to all the zinnias I've planted out, although I fear a young rabbit has chomped many of my young flowers in the front garden this season. It's very dispiriting. When one has spent so long dreaming and sowing and taking care of young plants, it's sad not to see them thriving and benefitting both you and the insect world. I should be picking armfuls of flowers to enjoy in the house and it just isn't happening. It's hard not to feel slightly cheated by the weather.

The hens have been feeling the heat too, walking around with their wings out and their beaks open. We fill a trug full of cold water to act as a paddling pool for them, but they need a little encouragement so we pick each girl up and give her a gentle dunk. This is meant to be especially beneficial for our big Brahma, Perdita, who has feathery feet, but she doesn't look impressed when we gently lower her in. The next day, though, we're thrilled to see a couple of the ex-bat girls hopping in all by themselves.

On most days, I seek the shade of our apple tree, taking my notebooks and pens with me. I love gazing up into the sky through the branches above me. The apples are swelling in size now, promising wonderful things in the kitchen come the autumn when the Aga is switched back on. But it's much too hot to think about the Aga today.

This summer, I've bought four scented pelargoniums. Each has leaves that smell fabulous and they seem to be thriving in the heat. I'm particularly in love with Cy's Sunburst whose scent is a very strong citrus, and Attar of Roses, the leaves of which made a delicious cup of tea the other night. I think scented pelargoniums could easily become a new obsession.

Rain is forecast and we rush around pulling out every trug and bucket we have to capture the precious water but, when we check on them later, we have hardly a drop. We have several plants like pitcher plants and blueberries that prefer rainwater and so it's important we have a constant supply. But the brief shower has barely penetrated the earth and everything needs a really good soaking.

The other worry we have is living in a thatched cottage. The roof will be extremely dry and it would only take a tiny spark from a piece of flying ash from someone's bonfire or summer barbecue and we'd be in trouble.

Once the heatwave has abated, we can enjoy summer again. There is nothing quite like stepping out into a warm summer morning. I let the hens out, change their water, check their food supply, collect the eggs, clean out the coop and make sure everyone looks healthy and happy. I open the greenhouse, breathing in that wondrous smell of things growing, and then give everything a good soak. If it's going to be a particularly hot day, I'll water the floor too in order to cool everything down.

This year, on a trip to the sea, we bought a children's fishing net to keep in the greenhouse as we often find ourselves struggling to rescue bees and butterflies who come in but can't seem to get out again. They can often exhaust themselves in the heat and it's heartbreaking to find their little broken bodies if they've failed to find their way to freedom. One trick I learned out of desperation before we bought our net was to use a brightly coloured flower which I'd hold up in order to entice the bee. I've succeeded in rescuing many bees this way – they land on the flower and I calmly walk to the door with them.

Another favourite morning task of mine is to walk around the garden simply looking. My right thumbnail is usually on high alert at this point, eager for some deadheading, and there are usually a few cosmos flowers or roses that require attention. This is my time for seeing what needs doing. Is there anything that needs staking? Have any plants finished their cycle and need cutting back? Do any seeds need to be collected? And, as with the hens, is everything healthy and happy? I also usually have my camera with me to capture the daily changes in the garden – a certain slant of light on a newly-opened bloom, perhaps, or the precise moment the first hollyhock reaches the thatched roof. I love documenting life at Old Thatch in this way.

But the weather is a real concern and, as July turns to August, we still see no rain. Every day is spent watering the garden, just trying to keep everything alive. I never thought I'd be praying for rain in the summer, but it really could make a difference.

Summer Party

When we lived at Mulberry Cottage, we used to host an annual Christmas party for artist friends, neighbours and collectors. Roy would spend a day in the kitchen making heaps of mince pies. We'd have mulled wine, decorate the cottage with a Christmas tree and lots of holly and ivy, light pretty candles and make sure the wood burner was going. It was always a lovely event. Our tiny cottage really leant itself to a winter gathering around the fireplace. But Old Thatch feels more of a summer venue to me and, in the times of Covid, we feel it makes sense to enjoy the fresh air of the garden, flinging open the conservatory doors and the French doors into the dining room. Guests will be able to drift in and out to look at Roy's paintings, flip through my books, and take drinks and cake out into the garden.

But the garden isn't looking as glorious as I hoped it would. The drifts of pink and white cosmos I've planted in the front garden are horribly stunted, reaching only half the height they should. The ammi majus and sweet peas are long over, both dried to a crisp in the heat, and the roses are resting between flushes. I console myself with the fact that everyone's gardens are struggling this summer. Besides, Old Thatch cheers me up by providing us with a second flowering of the wisteria. There's also a fabulous oak-leaved hydrangea which is in full bloom, and the apple tree is laden with fruit and looking lush and lovely.

So we get to work. We want everything to be light and sparkly for summer so Roy makes his award-winning Victoria sandwich which scooped him the WI shield for baking at our old village show. I make a lemon drizzle cake which also won first prize one year, and I add a chocolate orange drizzle to the medley because one must always have chocolate. We keep drinks simple with rose lemonade, elderflower cordial and a herby cola. Soft drinks for a warm summer's day.

A warm summer's day. That's what we expect because of the long, warm days we've had all summer but, as we check the weather forecast the week before, our hearts sink. Rain is forecast – the rain we've been praying for all summer and that hasn't arrived is now due on the very day we've chosen for our garden party. I can't believe it. We try not to panic. Weather forecasts can often change or be wrong. But we make a contingency plan so that guests will be able to come inside more. Not ideal. I'd wanted to drift around the garden in a light summer dress, scattering cushions everywhere and chatting under the apple tree.

Luckily, when the day itself arrives, we experience only one brief shower around lunchtime. The rest of the day is dry. There are clouds for some of it but sunshine too. At one point, it really gets quite hot. But it's so lovely to celebrate our work and garden with our new neighbours. This is only our second summer here and we're just beginning to form friendships.

What I love about parties is the way people find each other and, towards the end of the day, we have a lovely blend of friends from our old village and ones from our new one. We are all sitting under the apple tree; the shade is light and dappled in the late afternoon sun. It's a luxuriously lazy moment after a busy day and, perhaps, the first time Roy and I have sat down together with our guests.

We talk about our art, our inspirations, and we chat about the struggles everyone's had with their gardens this summer. We also talk about pigs. One villager remembers an old lady who lived in our cottage many years ago and who kept pigs in our back garden. This kind of conversation makes me very happy indeed and I feel that I've found exactly the right place in the world.

I look up at the cottage from under the apple tree and then back again at my dear friends and I smile. I'm happy here. Truly happy. There have been some difficult days since we moved to Old Thatch – days that were a real struggle to get through. But, with good friends and neighbours and a home we love, we know that life is good.

Victoria's Favourite Gardens

Here are a few gardens that have given me a lot of joy over the years and are definitely worth a visit if you're in the area:

Wimpole, Cambridgeshire
Blickling Hall, Norfolk
Felbrigg Hall, Norfolk
Helmingham Hall, Suffolk
Ickworth, Suffolk
Beeleigh Abbey, Essex
Bateman's, East Sussex
Perch Hill, East Sussex
Sissinghurst, Kent
Great Dixter, Kent
Rousham, Oxfordshire
Haddon Hall, Derbyshire
Chatsworth, Derbyshire
Attingham Park, Shropshire
Wallington, Northumberland

A lot of these gardens are owned by the National Trust but there are many other smaller, private gardens you can visit in the UK as part of the National Garden Scheme. These can feel wonderfully intimate and are just as inspirational as the larger gardens, if not more so, because it's easier to imagine achieving the same results in your own garden. You may also notice that many on this list are in East Anglia as this is where I have spent much of my life and so they are easily accessible to me. But there are so many wonderful gardens across the country – large and small, formal and wild, and it's one of the great joys of life to make your own discoveries.

Victoria's Favourite Garden Books

A Woman's Garden by Tanya Anderson
Floret Farm's Cut Flower Garden by Erin Benzakein and Julie Chai
Flourish by Willow Crossley
The Cut Flower Patch by Louise Curley
The Jewel Garden by Monty and Sarah Don
The Magic Apple Tree by Susan Hill
Creative Vegetable Gardening by Joy Larkcom
The Flower Farmer's Year by Georgie Newbery
From Seed to Bloom by Milli Proust
Elizabeth and her German Garden by Elizabeth Von Arnim
The Virago Book of Women Gardeners

End of Book Two

Acknowledgements

With thanks to Celia Hart and Catriona Robb for their contributions to this book. And special thanks to Anne-Marie and all my Suffolk friends and neighbours for making life so sweet. And, as ever, heartfelt thanks to Roy for always being there.

About the Author

Victoria Connelly is the bestselling author of *The Rose Girls* and *The Book Lovers* series.

With over a million sales, her books have been translated into many languages. The first, *Flights of Angels*, was made into a film in Germany. Victoria flew to Berlin to see it being made and even played a cameo role in it.

A Weekend with Mr Darcy, the first in her popular Austen Addicts series about fans of Jane Austen has sold over 100,000 copies. She is also the author of several romantic comedies including *The Runaway Actress* which was nominated for the Romantic Novelists' Association's Best Romantic Comedy of the Year.

Victoria was brought up in Norfolk, England before moving to Yorkshire where she got married in a medieval castle. After 11 years in London, she moved to rural Suffolk where she lives in a pink thatched cottage with her artist husband, a springer spaniel and her ex-battery hens.

To hear about future releases and receive a **free ebook** sign up for her newsletter at www.victoriaconnelly.com.

Also by Victoria Connelly

The House in the Clouds Series

The House in the Clouds
High Blue Sky
The Colour of Summer

The Book Lovers Series

The Book Lovers
Rules for a Successful Book Club
Natural Born Readers
Scenes from a Country Bookshop
Christmas with the Book Lovers

Other Books

The Beauty of Broken Things
One Last Summer
The Heart of the Garden
Love in an English Garden
The Rose Girls
The Secret of You

The Wrong Ghost

Christmas at The Cove

Christmas at the Castle

Christmas at the Cottage

A Summer to Remember

Wish You Were Here

The Runaway Actress

Molly's Millions

Flights of Angels

Irresistible You

Three Graces

A Weekend with Mr Darcy

The Perfect Hero (Dreaming of Mr Darcy)

Mr Darcy Forever

Christmas With Mr Darcy

Happy Birthday Mr Darcy

At Home with Mr Darcy

Escape to Mulberry Cottage (non-fiction)

A Year at Mulberry Cottage (non-fiction)

Summer at Mulberry Cottage (non-fiction)

Finding Old Thatch (non-fiction)

Book One in the Old Thatch series

Having left the busy London suburbs and moved to a village in rural Suffolk, author Victoria Connelly thought all her dreams had come true. But after nine years, it's time to leave Mulberry Cottage for a new adventure.

Victoria and her husband are absolutely *not* looking for a thatched cottage but, when they discover Old Thatch, they completely fall under its spell. With its five-hundred year old beams, wisteria-clad walls and pretty cottage garden, it's the perfect country retreat. But what's life really like in a listed building with sloping floors, wonky windows and a roof made of straw?

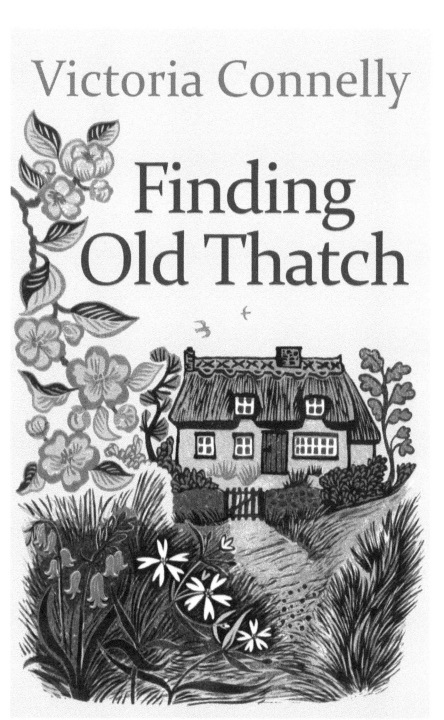

Victoria Connelly

Finding Old Thatch

If you have enjoyed reading about life at Old Thatch, you might also enjoy the Mulberry Cottage series of ebooks.

Swapping the London suburbs for a slice of country life...

Having grown up in rural Norfolk, author Victoria Connelly never thought she'd ever live in London but, after surviving eleven years in the noisy suburbs, she finally persuades her husband to move to Suffolk – to a county with no motorways, a village with no shops and a cottage with no mains drainage. Escape to Mulberry Cottage follows Victoria and her artist husband, Roy, as they embrace country life with their ever-expanding family of animals. Illustrated with twenty stunning photographs, it's the perfect read for anyone who has ever dreamed of getting away from it all.

Praise for Victoria Connelly's Mulberry Cottage Series:

'Enchanting.' - Erica James

'Victoria Connelly is writing in the tradition of Miss Read and bringing the pleasures of the countryside to a whole new generation.'
- Leah Fleming

Escape to
Mulberry
Cottage

Swapping the
London suburbs
for a slice of
country life

Victoria Connelly

Ingram Content Group UK Ltd.
Milton Keynes UK
UKHW021511260323
419096UK00010B/126